Crusade
Evangelism
and the
Local Church

Crusade Evangelism and the Local Church

Sterling W. Huston

World Wide

A ministry of the Billy Graham Association

1303 Hennepin Avenue
Minneapolis, Minnesota 55403

Acknowledgments

Bible verses marked KJV are taken from the King James Version of the Bible. Bible verses marked NIV are taken by permission from The Holy Bible, New International Version, copyright © 1978 International Bible Society, East Brunswick, New Jersey. Bible verses marked RSV are taken by permission from The Revised Standard Version Bible, copyrighted 1946, 1952, © 1971, 1973 National Council of the Churches of Christ in the U.S.A., New York, New York. Bible verses marked NASB are taken by permission from the New American Standard Bible, © The Lockman Foundation 1960, 1962, 1963, 1968, 1971, 1972, 1973, 1975, 1977, La Habra, California. Bible verses marked Williams are taken by permission from *The New Testament in the Language of the People,* by Charles B. Williams, copyright renewed 1956 Edith S. Williams, Moody Press, Chicago, Illinois. Bible verses marked TLB are taken by permission from *The Living Bible,* © 1971 Tyndale House Publishers, Wheaton, Illinois.

Library of Congress Catalog Card Number: 83-050462
ISBN 0-89066-048-4

Crusade Evangelism and the Local Church, by Sterling W. Huston, © 1984 Billy Graham Evangelistic Association. Published by World Wide Publications, 1303 Hennepin Avenue, Minneapolis, Minnesota 55403, U.S.A.

First published 1984
Reprinted 1986

Printed in the United States of America

Dedication

To my wife, Esther, and our children, Todd and Alissa, who have lovingly supported me in the ministry of evangelism, and who have willingly given up their time with me in order that this book may be written.

Contents

Foreword

My first crusade was in 1939 in a small Baptist church in Palatka, Florida. Following that, I held a number of campaigns (as we called them in those days) in many churches, both in the north and the south. I am sure the sermons were very poor and the invitation was often confused—but I tried to preach with the same vigor, earnestness, and dedication that I do now. Mainly I had zeal—but not much knowledge about evangelism, particularly at first.

My first city-wide campaign was in Grand Rapids, Michigan. It was the first of many campaigns that would take us to various places in the United States, and in 1946 the Lord opened the door for us to go to Great Britain for six months of evangelistic campaigns. One of the most important things that happened to us during those early years was that God drew together several people—such as Cliff Barrows (and his wife, Billie, who was our pianist) and George Beverly Shea. They formed the nucleus of our team. I began then to realize the way God has given specific gifts to various individuals, and that the God-given gift of the evangelist is most effective when it is practiced in close harmony with the other gifts God has given to His people.

As time went along and our opportunities grew, I began to realize the great need for careful advance preparations and follow-up to united evangelistic efforts. God brought across our path several individuals who were used by Him to help us in this critical area. The man who taught us more about evangelism than probably anyone else was Willis Haymaker. In those days evangelism was often associated with excessive emotion, an anti-intellectual approach, or a non-co-operative attitude toward other Christians. Upon Willis' advice, we changed "campaigns" to "crusades" and determined to work in close cooperation with churches wherever possible. He also helped us lay the foundation for careful Crusade preparations so that churches would be mobilized to reach their communities for Christ. More than that, Willis Haymaker impressed upon us the central role that prayer must play in evangelism.

Another man whom God sent across our path was Dawson Trotman, the founder and leader of The Navigators, who came to help us with our counseling and follow-up programs. We had sensed for some time that follow-up was often the weakest link in Crusade evangelism, and Dawson took the lead in developing the methods that would later be refined and become such an important part of our ministry. During our London Crusade in Harringay Arena (1954), Cliff Barrows, other members of our team, and I had almost become exhausted trying to do as much counseling as possible after each night's service. Dawson came to me and said, "Don't you believe that God has given *us* gifts too? Your gift is platform preaching. Let us handle the counseling of those who come forward." This taught us a great lesson—to recognize the gifts God has given to others and to delegate responsibility to them.

As times have changed we have tried hard—and with much prayer—to adapt and revise the methods we have learned over nearly four decades of Crusade evangelism. We have made many mistakes—but we have always tried to learn from our mistakes. I thank God for the uncounted men and women He has used over the years to help us and teach us to be more effective in reaching our world for Christ.

Dr. Sterling Huston is now Director of our North American Crusades, working with a fine staff of gifted and committed individuals who assist in organizing the myriad details that are part of a large city Crusade. Their commitment to evangelism, their insight and wisdom, and their practical experience make them what I believe to be the most magnificent band of men and women who have ever been involved in this particular method of evangelism.

In this book Dr. Huston sums up the principles and practical methods that have been developed across the years by all those who have helped us. Sterling and his associates have first-hand knowledge of the inner workings of our ministry. He expresses them with clarity and conviction, stressing that evangelism is more than methods which may change as circumstances change. Evangelism is the proclamation of the Gospel of Jesus Christ—a timeless and unchanging message that alone is "the power of God unto salvation to everyone that believeth" (Romans 1:16, KJV). At the same time (as Sterling vividly shows) God can use methods as tools to break through the barriers of indifference, ignorance, and hostility that keep so many from the Gospel. I commend Sterling Huston and all who have assisted him in preparing this book.

As I have read it, I have been challenged to increase my own commitment to evangelism. While the book basically concentrates on the specific ministry of our organization, it is my hope that it will be helpful to both clergy and laymen who seek a better understanding of the principles and practices of evangelism today—whatever the method might be. The principles have been tested in Crusades around the world, and their application is universal. They also can be valuable in making other methods of evangelism more effective as well.

It is my prayer that this book will not only inform you, but that it will inspire you and challenge you as you seek to fulfill our Lord's command to "go into all the world and preach the good news to all creation" (Mark 16:15, NIV).

—Billy Graham

Introduction

"DO THE WORK OF AN EVANGELIST"! This slogan was arrayed in huge bold banners across the assembly hall of Amsterdam's Rai Centre as some 5,000 evangelists and Christian workers from 133 nations gathered for ten historic days in July of 1983. Again and again, through addresses, media displays, printed materials and music, this message resounded thunderously like a drum beat on the consciousness of the delegates as the central theme of the International Conference for Itinerant Evangelists known as Amsterdam 83. This commission from Paul raises two questions: what is the work of the evangelist, and how do you do it—effectively? This book will address these questions, among others.

For over twenty-five years I have been involved in various ministries of evangelism; twenty of those years have been with the Billy Graham Evangelistic Association. Throughout this time my perspective on evangelism has been shaped by personal experience with a wide variety of methods and through a multitude of discussions—both sympathetic and unsympathetic—with clergymen, seminary professors, denominational leaders and hundreds of lay Christians. The diversity of opinion and perspective on evangelism revealed in these discussions has been enlightening to say the least. It has taught me (or at least has begun to teach me) how limited, and in some cases distorted, our concepts of evangelism are. The obvious need to clarify the goals of evangelism and to identify the means to reach those goals has motivated me to commit to writing some of the lessons learned.

One of the lessons is in priorities. Evangelism must

be a passion before it becomes a program. A Holy-Spirit inspired sense of mission precedes the choice of a method to fulfill that mission. The Bible does not spend much time describing specific methods, but it is clear on the mission, the message, and the motivation of evangelism. Like many other aspects of Scripture, the choice of method is or should be guided by biblical principles.

In my years of involvement in evangelism, I have encountered certain biblical principles that are crucial to its success. An adequate understanding of these is important to any form of evangelism and, in particular, Crusade evangelism. The saying is true: "Methods are many, principles are few; methods often change, but principles never do." For this reason I have chosen to write a book not so much of procedures and methods but rather of principles which determine the methods used in evangelism. These basic evangelism principles will be illustrated from Crusade situations with two objectives in mind:

1. to permit those who have the opportunity for Crusade evangelism to participate more effectively;
2. to help the local church become more effective in all forms of evangelism through a proper understanding and application of these principles.

Although this book deals primarily with Billy Graham Crusades, my intent is to show that all evangelism is built on biblical principles which may be implemented through a variety of methods. These principles, illustrated through Crusade evangelism, may be applied to small group, neighborhood, personal and single-church outreach. As such, what happens in a Billy Graham Crusade can happen in many other settings. Even though your opportunity may be different in its magnitude, methods, and messenger, you can experience the same results—people being converted to Christ!

The bottom line is this: a clear understanding of these principles and a proper application of them in your setting will result in effective evangelism. It is my prayer that the contents of these pages will both encourage and enhance the work of local churches and individual Christians in fulfilling our Lord's Great Commission to "go and make disciples of all nations" (Matthew 28:19, NIV).

Although it has been my privilege and responsibility to explain our ministry of Crusade evangelism in writing, in the truest sense this is not my book. First, it represents the evolution of Crusade methodology which has developed over more than thirty-five years of Billy Graham's ministry. Such men as Willis Haymaker, Dawson Trotman, Walter Smyth, and Charlie Riggs have played both a pioneering and a prominent role in shaping and refining the Crusade process. Second, it represents the beneficial influence of many others in this ministry upon my life, and my understanding of Crusade evangelism for over twenty years. Among them are Cliff Barrows, John Corts, John Dillon and our Crusade Directors. But most important, this book emanates from the priorities, preaching, and person of Billy Graham, who has shaped this ministry and who has graciously encouraged me in the writing of this book.

Many others have played an important role in this effort. Among them are John Wesley White whose research assistance and encouragement have been very helpful, and Roger C. Palms whose advice and editorial guidance have been invaluable. I have further benefited from the constructive suggestions of John Akers, Lewis Drummond, Jim Douglas, Leighton Ford, Peter Wagner, and Sherwood E. Wirt. Especially helpful have been the copy editing of Kersten Beckstrom and the publishing assistance of DeWayne Herbrandson and Kathy Ganz. And I cannot speak too highly of the excellent work done by my administrative assistant, Cathy Wood, who coordinated the many details involved in the research for and typing of the manuscript supported by our Team Office staff who so efficiently provided secretarial services.

My appreciation is deepest for my wife, Esther, and our two children, Todd and Alissa, who have encouraged me in this task even though it required many hours away from them. It is because of their love, prayers and sense of shared calling to the ministry of evangelism that I have been able to engage freely in this effort.

Ultimately, my gratitude and praise is for my Lord Jesus Christ, whose Gospel this book proclaims and whose kingdom it seeks to extend with the prayer that these pages will hasten the day of His return.

1

Proclamation:

The Evangelist's Ministry and Message

According to the U.S. Weather Bureau, it was the worst rain storm to hit New England since 1906. It had been raining all weekend and now on the closing Sunday of the Crusade, June 6, 1982, the driving rain was more intense than ever. In spite of conditions which would have caused almost any other outdoor event to be canceled, some 19,000 persons gathered at Nickerson Field on the campus of Boston University. The sea of faces were virtually hidden by rain-hats, raincoats, and umbrellas, as the crowds of people sat on chairs, bleachers, and even on the wet artificial turf which in some places was covered by several inches of water that had accumulated over the weekend.

Billy Graham was preaching, holding his Bible aloft and pressing his points home with his hand gestures, seemingly oblivious to the driving rain. His message was authoritative, simple, urgent—the style so familiar to millions. All week long his appeal to the audiences had been direct, "Jesus Christ can meet your need. You may be lonely. You may feel empty. You may have guilt. You may be fearful. Come to Christ. He understands! He'll forgive you. He'll bring salvation and peace into your life." Despite the nearly impossible conditions Billy Graham was still proclaiming the Gospel of Christ with undiminished fervor and spiritual power.

What makes a man stand out in the driving rain, preaching to thousands? It wasn't the size of the crowd. Billy Graham had preached to much larger audiences—1,100,000 in Korea in May of 1973; 225,000 in Maracana Stadium in Rio de Janeiro in 1974—and even in this same city 50,000 had gathered on the Boston Common during a previous Crusade in 1950. And it wasn't the uniqueness of the opportunity. After thirty-five years of preaching the Gospel under almost every conceivable circumstance and to every imaginable audience, this certainly was not a unique occasion. Then what was the compelling force? Why wasn't Billy Graham at home, relaxing beside a pleasant fire in the hearth with his slippered feet up? What was he doing in Boston in the rain, preaching with the intensity of a first sermon and with the urgency of a last one?

This kind of commitment doesn't just happen. Billy Graham was called to be an evangelist, and his convictions about preaching the Gospel have been forged over years of study and prayer. They have been deepened and reinforced by the unusual blessing of God upon his ministry. But he has had to answer some hard questions: "What is the evangelist's ministry?" "What is the message of the Gospel?" "How should it be preached?" "What about the invitation?" These pages will seek to address the issues which are critical to effective Crusade evangelism.

The Evangelist's Ministry

The ministry of the evangelist is best understood by looking first at his gift and then his task. The New Testament reveals that when Christ ascended, He "gave gifts to men . . . some to be evangelists" (Ephesians 4:8, 11, NIV). This gift from Christ to His church was given for a specific task. Paul exhorted Timothy about this task when he wrote, "Do the work of an evangelist" (2 Timothy 4:5, NIV). As Stephen F. Olford has pointed out, "The noun 'evangelist' comes from the verb 'to announce the good news'; in simple terms, therefore, the evangelist is the herald or announcer of the good news of the Gospel. Whether in public preaching or in personal counseling, the task of the evangelist is 'so to present Christ in the power of the Holy Spirit that men [and women] shall come to put their trust in God through Him, to accept Him as their Savior, and serve Him as their King in the fellowship of His church.' "[1] Professor of Evangelism Richard Peace affirmed this task of the evangelist when he said, "This gift consists of the special ability to share the Gospel message with unbelievers in such a way that they understand who Jesus is and are moved to commit themselves to Him."[2]

We further clarify the evangelist's ministry when we understand what evangelism is. The Lausanne Covenant defines it this way:

> "To evangelize is to spread the good news that Jesus Christ died for our sins and was raised from the dead according to the Scriptures, and that as the reigning Lord He now offers the forgiveness of sins and the liberating gift of the Spirit to all who repent and believe. . . . Evangelism itself is the proclamation of the historical, biblical Christ as Savior and Lord, with a view to persuading people to come to Him personally and so be reconciled to God. In issuing the Gospel invitation we have no liberty to conceal the cost of discipleship. . . . The results of evangelism include obedience to Christ, incorporation into His church and responsible service in the world."[3]

Billy Graham emphasizes that he did not seek the gift of an evangelist. This was given by the Holy Spirit, just as the Holy Spirit appoints all the gifts listed in Scripture. Having received the gift, it is his responsibility, as with all evangelists, to fulfill its ministry. Billy Graham interprets his role as "a communicator of the Gospel, an announcer of the good news." He points out that "whereas a pastor can use a shotgun and cover the whole range of Christian doctrine, an evangelist shoots primarily with a rifle." His principle message is the Gospel.

Difficulties arise when evangelists stray from their calling and begin to take on the responsibilities of other gifted members of the body. Years ago Billy Graham concluded that his primary role is not to be pastor, though he has pastored; not to be an educator, though he was president of a college; not to be an administrator, though he does administrate; and not to be a social activist, though he has a strong social conscience.

Sometimes other well-meaning members of the Body of Christ want the highly visible evangelist to carry out their calling as well as his own. It is not healthy for the physical body to ask the mouth to do the work of the hands. Likewise, it is not healthy for the Body of Christ to ask one member with a particular gift to attempt to fulfill the work of another member who has a different gift. This divides the focus and dilutes effectiveness. If it is appropriate to ask the vocational evangelist to be equally visible and active in the social application of the Gospel, then it is also appropriate to ask the social activist to be equally active and visible in the work of winning souls. Aiming at two separate targets with the same bullet usually means missing both objects.

Leighton Ford aptly points out that the reason for Billy Graham's effectiveness as an evangelist is "an unswerving dedication to the primary call of declaring Christ. Billy Graham has sometimes been accused of narrowness. But much of his secret has been the focusing of all his powers upon one task. . . . He has resisted all sorts of tempting offers to go on to politics or to become an entertainer. He has refused those who would turn him into a professional anti-Communist or a race crusader. Part of the power of his preaching lies in the intensity of purpose, which is the thrust of every sermon from start to finish: so to present Christ that men must decide."[4]

The Evangelist's Message

The biblical role of the evangelist determines the message that he preaches. When Billy Graham preached in London for twelve weeks in 1954, an Anglican clergyman came to him and said, "Mr. Graham, I attended every night for three months, and you preached the same sermon every night." Mr. Graham said later, "I thought I had preached a different sermon every night, but I knew what he meant. He meant that certain things have to be said in every Gospel message, because it is the Gospel. There has to be the love of God; there has to be the cross of Jesus; there has to be the resurrection of Christ; there has to be the fact of sin and man's response by repentance and faith. All of that has to come into every message. I try to use different illustrations and different biblical backgrounds, but the message of the Gospel is the same."

The content of the evangelist's message has long been a subject for debate. C. H. Dodd in his helpful and clarifying volume, *The Apostolic Preaching and Its Development*, has made a clear distinction between the *didache* or teaching ministry of the early church and the *kerygma* which was the "public proclamation of Christianity to the non-Christian world."[5]

"What then was the essence of this proclamation by the original heralds of the faith? Quite briefly it was this. They proclaimed that prophecy was fulfilled; that in Jesus of Nazareth, in His words and deeds, His life, death and resurrection, the new age had arrived; that God had exalted Him, that He would come again as Judge, and that now was the day of salvation. This was the message."[6]

Speaking to more than 4,000 evangelists at Amsterdam in 1983, Billy Graham declared, "Jesus is the message. Jesus Christ, by His death and resurrection, became the Gospel. It is not a new set of morals or a guide for happy living. It's the solemn message that we're alienated from God, and only Christ, by His death and resurrection, can save us."[7] Paul sums up the message in these words: "I want to remind you of the gospel I preached to you. . . . By this gospel you are saved . . . that Christ died for our sins according to the Scriptures, that he was buried, that he was raised on the third day according to the Scriptures" (1 Corinthians 15:1-4, NIV).

In recent years Billy Graham has increasingly emphasized the cost of following Christ. He told evangelists at Amsterdam, "During the past three or four years, I have noticed a new emphasis in my own ministry. That emphasis is on discipleship. The Gospel is *simple*, but His demands of self-denying and cross-bearing are difficult. We have no right to offer a cheaper Gospel and make it easier for anyone."[8]

Perhaps Billy Graham's message can best be summed up by his comment to the press before the 1954 Harringay meetings in London. He said, "I am going to present a God who matters, and who makes claims on the human race. He is a God of love, grace, and mercy, but also a God of judgment. When we break His moral laws, we suffer; when we keep them, we have inward peace and joy. . . . I am calling for a revival that will cause men and women to return to their offices and shops to live out the teaching of Christ in their daily relationships. I am going to preach a Gospel not of despair but of hope—hope for the individual, for society, and for the world."[9]

Some clergymen feel that Crusade evangelism does not give enough emphasis to the social applications of the Gospel. Leighton Ford, in his book *The Christian Persuader*, says, "Critics have attacked evangelistic campaigns for a lack of permanent results, but the scholarly works of men like Timothy Smith, J. Edwin Orr, Kenneth Scott Latourette, John Wesley White, and others have amply documented the impact of this kind of evangelism on social reform, world missions, church growth, and Christian unity.

"Those who say that mass evangelism has not been involved with, nor concerned about, social problems should read their history again. Admittedly, some evangelists have been unconcerned about the social problems of the day. But a careful reading of history shows that many social movements were directly related to persons motivated through evangelistic activity.

"Charles Finney took a strong stand with the antislavery movement and set in motion currents which issued in important eventualities. Interdenominational temperance societies in Britain began in 1830 when a Bradford merchant was spurred by Lyman Beecher's sermons. Elizabeth Fry, the pioneer of prison reform, was inspired by Stephen Grollet of Philadelphia. Elihu Burritt felt Christians should seek to outlaw war forever and his efforts on both sides of the Atlantic form an epic. For over a century the Salvation Army has espoused the cause of the 'submerged tenth.' Dr. Thomas Barnardo, whose homes have set up a chain reaction of caring for derelict children, was converted under the ministry of the California evangelist, John Hambleton. Keir Hardie, who was chiefly responsible for the British Labor Party of 1900, was a convert of D. L. Moody and became an evangelist in the ranks of the Evangelical Union, itself a result of Finney's revivals, before entering the field of politics.

To the end Hardie maintained his Christian profession, expending his efforts selflessly for the alleviation of poverty.''[10]

The distinction, as well as the relationship, between proclamation and application of the Gospel was clearly made in The Lausanne Covenant:

> "Although reconciliation with man is not reconciliation with God, nor is social action evangelism, nor is political liberation salvation, nevertheless we affirm that evangelism and sociopolitical involvement are both part of our Christian duty."[11]

Leighton Ford put this in perspective when he said, "We can expect the power of the kingdom to bring some profound and positive changes of peace, justice, and freedom in the structures of our world. And we should pray and work to that end. But primary in Jesus' program is the changing of men and women. Christian social and political action are imperative, but it is folly to think that the world will be changed without changing people."

The evangelist is particularly gifted to make clear the Gospel and to call people to a commitment to Christ. Although he will speak out on the responsibility to apply the grace of God to the needs of society, that is not his primary task. His calling is to make clear to persons everywhere that reconciliation with God is not only necessary but possible through Jesus Christ.

How Should the Message Be Preached?

Billy Graham, who has preached to more people face to face than anyone else in the history of Christianity, was asked at Amsterdam 83 to share his convictions on how the Gospel should be preached. He emphasized three points:

> "*First, the message must be preached with authority.* Preach it with conviction and assurance, knowing

that 'faith comes from hearing the message, and the message is heard through the word of Christ' (Romans 10:17, NIV). At one time in my life I had a struggle believing the Bible to be the authoritative Word of God. Some professors and other intellectuals were talking about their doubts and showing me what they claimed were contradictions in the Bible. I was young and had just gotten out of school and was having my first experiences in preaching. I began to doubt.

"So I went into the mountains, laid my Bible on the stump of a tree, and I said, 'Oh, Lord, I do not understand everything in this Book, but I accept it by faith as Your Word.' And I want to tell you I have never had a doubt since then. When I quote the Scriptures, I know I am quoting the Word of God. The Bible is God's authoritative message to us. It is an infallible Book. Let us never depart from that.

"Do you preach with authority? That is absolutely essential to the communication of the Gospel. One reason the people listened to Jesus was that He spoke 'as one having authority' (Matthew 7:29, KJV). When you quote God's Word, He will use it. He will never allow it to return void.

"*Second, the message must be preached with simplicity.* One of the temptations in preaching to audiences is to try to speak to the intellectuals in the group. When we try to do that, the rest of the audience often misses our point. We must learn to take the profound things of God and proclaim them in simplicity. Our message should be so clear that children can understand it. Many pastors have discovered that when they give a children's message, the adults remember that better than the regular sermon. James Denney, the great Scottish preacher, once said, 'The man who shoots above the target does not prove thereby that he has superior ammunition. He just proves that he cannot shoot.'

"*Third, the message must be preached with urgency.*

We hold in our hands a life-and-death message, an eternal message. You may be speaking to some people who will be hearing the Gospel for the last time. It is the one message that can transform the world and our community, that can transform a family that is torn and broken and hurting. We need to preach for a decision. Psychologists have studied our Crusades, and although they have sometimes been critical of the music and the message, they have not been critical of the invitation. They have said that it is important for people to have a release in response to the message. That release comes when we offer them a time and a place to make a commitment. It doesn't have to be done just as we do it in large meetings, but there should be an opportunity for a decision. Only when we are preaching to reach a verdict will people sense our urgency."

And that is exactly what Billy Graham was doing on that rainy Sunday in Boston, and what he has always done, preaching the message of the Gospel with the authority of "the Bible says"; preaching it with simplicity so that a child can understand it; and preaching it with the urgency of a life-and-death message realizing that some people may be hearing it for the last time. The entire message is an invitation to come to Christ and be reconciled with God.

Why the Invitation?

In Billy Graham Crusades at the conclusion of the message an invitation is given, a simple appeal for people to make a commitment to Christ. The Holy Spirit may have used the message or some aspect of the service to speak to individuals about their need of forgiveness, of salvation, of assurance, of rededication of life, or of some other spiritual need. Whatever the reason, persons sensing their spiritual need are invited to leave their seats, walk forward, and stand in front of the platform. The evangelist gives them brief instructions and leads them in prayer. Then a trained counselor spends time with each inquirer, clarifying his decision and obtaining information for follow-up purposes. The inquirers leave that night with a Bible study and other materials to assist them in their new commitment and spiritual growth.

Biblical Basis

There is a biblical basis for the invitation. Whenever Jesus called someone to follow Him, He called that person publicly. Such statements as "follow Me" . . . "come after Me" . . . "take up your cross" . . . "forsake all that you have" . . . "come unto Me" were characteristic of Jesus' call to those who would be loyal to Him. He said, "Whosoever therefore shall confess me before men, him will I confess also before my Father which is in heaven" (Matthew 10:32, KJV). The apostle Peter, at the end of his first sermon preached after Pentecost, said, "Repent, and be baptized" (Acts 2:38, KJV). The apostle Paul reminded the Romans that "it is with your heart that you believe and are justified, and it is with your mouth that you confess and are saved" (Romans 10:10, NIV). Clearly, it is not enough merely to preach Christ. Men and women need to be invited to choose Him.

Historical Precedent

There is historical precedent for the current method of extending an invitation. The Gospel always contains an invitation to come to Christ and to follow Him, but the practical method of expressing that invitation is man-made. Wisdom and sensitivity from the Holy Spirit are needed in choosing the appropriate method in any given ministry setting. The preachers of the Gospel who have been earnest in their quest for souls have utilized various methods of public invitation from New Testament days until the present. Jonathan Edwards and George Whitefield invited "seekers" to come at another time for spiritual instruction. John Wesley first used the mourners' bench as a form of invitation. Finney asked the convicted persons to stand and come to the anxious seat. Booth and Spurgeon also invited "inquirers" to respond publicly. D. L. Moody and then R. A. Torrey had responders to "the invitation" come forward to an "inquiry room" where both "after meetings" and personal work was done one-to-one. Whether the invitation was issued every time, whether people were invited to the front of the church or auditorium or to some other room, an invitation was given because the preaching was for a verdict. People were asked to make a choice!

Psychological Reason

There is a psychological reason for giving an invitation. The evangelist has been preaching to the whole person—intellect, emotion, will—and God wants a response from the whole person. After listening with his mind, a person makes a decision to commit himself to Christ by his will. But that does not leave out emotions. Every human experience in life involves our emotions . . . birth, love, marriage, sickness, death, and success. There is a legitimate place for emotion in the preaching of the Gospel and in the response to that message. As Dr. John MacKay has said, "Something is wrong when emotion becomes legitimate in everything except religion."

The problem comes when emotions degenerate into emotionalism. Emotionalism has been defined as emotions out of control. When the invitation to receive Christ is given with integrity and without manipulation, it can actually help to avoid this problem of emotionalism. As George E. Sweazey said, "An emotion is saved from degenerating into emotionalism only by giving it some way of proper expression. The fear that giving an invitation in a public meeting may lead people to do something for which they are not ready must be balanced against the fear that not giving an invitation may keep people from doing something for which they are ready. That last may well do the greater psychic and spiritual damage. To stir people religiously without giving them anything they can do about it leaves them far worse off than they were before."[12]

Practical Reason

In Crusade evangelism there is also a practical reason for giving an invitation. When the Gospel is preached within the walls of a church, the hearer can make an appointment with the minister, or come back the next week and hear more. The church and the staff will still be there, and often classes are available to explain what it means to become a Christian. But when the Gospel is preached during a city-wide evangelistic Crusade, which is often held in the unique setting of a public auditorium or stadium, this is not possible. The inquirer who returns to the auditorium or stadium the next week may find an athletic event, a concert, or no activity at all; but he will probably not find an opportunity to respond to Christ nor will he likely find concerned and trained Christians to aid him in his commitment. By inviting people to come forward, the evangelist offers immediate spiritual help to inquirers, and counselors obtain important information which will assist in follow-up.

Dr. Helmut Thielicke, famed German preacher and theologian, sent a most moving and affirming letter to Billy Graham after attending the 1963 Crusade in Los Angeles. In particular, Thielicke addressed the matter of the invitation which he had been frankly critical of before coming to the services. He wrote, "I am speaking of the way in which you call people to come forward and to confirm their decision. It all happened without pressure and emotionalism (contrary to the reports which I had received up until now). It was far more the Shepherd's voice calling out in love and sorrow for the wandering ones.

"I saw them all coming toward us; I saw their assembled, moved and honestly decided faces; I saw their searching and their meditativeness. I confess that this moved me to the very limits. Above all, there were two young men—a white and a black—who stood at the front and about whom one felt that they were standing at that moment on Mount Horeb and looking from afar into a land that they had longed for. I shall never forget those faces. It became lightning clear that men want to make a decision."

Billy Graham's method is simple and straightforward. He begins the invitation at the start of his message. Often his opening remarks to the congregation are, "You are not here tonight by accident. I believe God has brought you here, and some of you need to find God tonight. You need to listen not only with your physical ears, but with your spiritual ears." Throughout the message he will say again and again, "You need to come to Christ; you need to place your faith in Christ; you need to commit your life to Christ; you can do that tonight." When Mr. Graham finishes his message, he continues that invitation by asking people from all over the auditorium or stadium to get up out of their seats and come to the front. There have been no emotional or death-bed stories throughout the preaching of the message. The invitation is without manipulation. He has been speaking about Jesus Christ and His ability to meet the deepest needs of people today. It is a simple, clear call to come to Christ.

A Presbyterian minister, who admittedly was fearful about the invitation and did not use this method in his own church services, wrote a letter expressing his feelings following the Crusade in his city.

"Watching [the invitation to 'come to Christ'], being a part of that, was one of the most awesome, exhilarating, and beautiful experiences that I have ever had. No pulling at heart strings, no tricking people or laying guilt trips on them. Just a simple, straightforward invitation to come to Christ and do business with Him. And then in the silence (though sometimes with music in the background), they came. By the hundreds and thousands. Young and old. There are no words to express my gratitude for the privilege of seeing their faces, of being there to watch and to counsel.

"There's no doubt about it. God was at work. I talked with many. People were sincerely and calmly doing business with God, 140 of them from my own congregation came forward; what a rich experience it has been to share their joy with them."

God was mightily at work in Boston despite the torrential rain of that Sunday afternoon, June 6. When the invitation was given, people streamed forward— the young, the old, the single, the married, the finely dressed and well-educated, the downtrodden and un-kempt, people with bewildered faces—from every walk of life. There was the middle-aged schoolteacher who went forward with his whole family and said, "I love God, but I don't know anything about Him." The whole family accepted Christ. There was the thirteen-year-old girl who went forward to give her heart to Christ. She said, "My father is a minister, but that doesn't help too much." And a thirty-eight-year-old accountant walked forward on the rain-soaked turf along with his wife to accept Christ. He was so excited that he exclaimed, "I'm going to read the Gospel of John on the train tonight." A Spanish-speaking woman said, "There is something missing in my heart, and I want it to be whole." She opened her heart to Christ.[13] Even the curious and nonreligious responded. A woman dressed in jeans, who obviously had not planned to attend a religious service, wandered into the meeting part way through and couldn't find a seat. She sat on the rain-soaked turf in front of the press table, seemingly oblivious to everything except the message. When the invitation was given, she was among the first to respond.

They came not because of a dynamic personality but because of the power of the Gospel. This was clearly demonstrated at Boston's Nickerson Field since the message was translated simultaneously into four different languages through use of a special AM frequency radio. Among those responding were people speaking each of those languages who had not heard the message in the words of Billy Graham but through the words of a translator. The response, obviously, is not the persuasion of a man, but the work of the Holy Spirit. As Billy Graham has so often quoted, "This is the Lord's doing; it is marvelous in our eyes" (Psalm 188:23, KJV).

In Review:

1. The evangelist's task is "the proclamation of the historical, biblical Christ as Savior and Lord, with a view to persuading people to come to Him personally and so be reconciled to God."[14] Although the evangelist will speak out on the responsibility to apply the grace of God to the needs of society, that is not his primary task.
2. The evangelist's message is necessarily a narrow one by definition of his task: "to spread the good news that Jesus Christ died for our sins and was raised from the dead according to the Scriptures, and . . . He now offers the forgiveness of sins . . . to all who repent and believe."[15]
3. The evangelist's message should be preached with authority, with simplicity, and with urgency.

4. The evangelist should preach for a verdict and invite people to respond to this good news. Although the method of inviting response may vary, depending upon circumstances, the invitation to come to Christ should always be part of the message.

2
Purpose:
Primary Objectives of Crusade Evangelism

Just before He ascended, Christ gave a mandate to His Church. The assurance of a promise and the assignment of a purpose were among Jesus' last words to His followers: "But ye shall receive power, after that the Holy Ghost is come upon you: and ye shall be witnesses unto me both in Jerusalem, and in all Judea, and in Samaria, and unto the uttermost part of the earth" (Acts 1:8, KJV). The *geographic scope* of that mandate to evangelize is clear—take this good news to your city (Jerusalem), to your country (Judea), to neighboring nations (Samaria), and to all people everywhere (the uttermost part of the earth). The promise of enabling power and the purpose of world evangelization are as valid today as when Jesus spoke the words nearly 2,000 years ago.

Purpose: The Goal of Evangelism

The *purpose* of the church's witness is further clarified by Jesus' words, "Therefore go and make disciples of all nations, baptizing them in the name of the Father and of the Son and of the Holy Spirit, and teaching them to obey everything I have commanded you" (Matthew 28:19, NIV). This command makes it clear that evangelism is a *means* and not an *end*. The aim of any evangelistic endeavor should go beyond making "decisions" to the making of "disciples." It is not the accumulation of attendance or response "statistics," but the developing of servants who are committed to Christ and to living out their commitment in a local church. As John Stott has pointed out, we achieve the goal of evangelism only ". . . by preaching the Gospel. For in preaching the Gospel we preach Christ so that men are converted to Him and become His disciples. We can never get away from, or grow out of, this elementary truth that evangelism is preaching Jesus Christ and making disciples of Jesus Christ."[1]

Although the "Great Commission" (Matthew 28:19–20) is well known by Christians, it is often misinterpreted. Discipleship leader Waldron Scott points out that most Christians see this essentially as a twofold commission: (1) to go (that is, to evangelize) and (2) to disciple (that is, to baptize converts and teach them). They assume a chronological sequence: evangelism first, followed by discipling. Such a reading, however prevalent, is unwarranted exegetically, as numerous biblical scholars have pointed out. The great Commission is unitary, not dualistic. Its primary, even sole, objective is discipleship."[2]

Scott further states, "Of course, it is not the evangelist's sole responsibility to 'make disciples' in any ultimate sense. . . . The evangelist is part of that larger team. He functions most productively when he integrates his efforts with those of the whole Body of Christ. By his own public commitment to discipling, however, the evangelist sets the tone of the total endeavor and stimulates churches to take seriously their responsibility to complete the discipling process."[3]

Not every "decision" means a "disciple," but that is more likely to be the end result if our ultimate goal is "making disciples." Since this is the emphasis of a Crusade, as much effort must be put into preparing for follow-up and the preservation of the results as is invested in the reaping of those results.

Some evangelistic ministries ignore or are oblivious to the clear teaching of the Great Commission. Claiming great numbers of decisions, they make little or no effort to integrate them into the life of local churches. The result, five to ten years later, is that there is little evidence of any remaining fruit. This often results in disillusionment to the local church, damage to individuals who "made decisions," and ultimately discouragement to the leaders of that ministry. Such ministries need to reevaluate their message and methods in light of Christ's clear mandate to "make disciples."

Conversely, other evangelism ministries are overly cautious and refuse to sow the good seed of the Gospel until all their discipling programs are in place. As commendable as this seems, such an approach can place too much emphasis on man's judgment as to when "all things are ready" and upon man's ability to conserve the fruit of the harvest. Inadvertently, this approach can hinder an effort of generous sowing and thus prevent bountiful reaping (2 Corinthians 9:6). Either approach can hinder or limit the work of the Great Commission. The responsible evangelist wants to see disciples, but sows generously in obedience to Christ, whether or not he is permitted to reap where he has sown or to see disciples from the harvest. With a clear commitment to making disciples and preparing the church for that process, we must still remember that Jesus commissioned us to "go . . . into all the world, and preach the gospel to every creature" (Mark 16:15, KJV).

Objectives of Crusade Evangelism

Crusade evangelism seeks to fulfill the mandate of "making disciples" through two primary objectives:

1. *To evangelize the community:* The first objective of Crusade evangelism is to proclaim the Gospel of Jesus Christ in the power of the Holy Spirit, to invite men and

women to commit their lives to Christ, and to relate those who respond to a local church for continuing spiritual nurture and discipleship. The target area is the whole community or metropolitan area. Crusade evangelism utilizes many methods starting before the public meetings begin and continuing long after they are completed. Billy Graham has emphasized that personal evangelism is the most effective form of evangelism, and that a large evangelistic gathering is successful only when substantial personal evangelism has already taken place.

The effect of this emphasis is felt by the local church both before and following the Crusade meetings. A past president of the American Baptist Churches, Dr. Roger Fredrikson, reported that when a Crusade came to his city, more persons made professions of faith in his Sunday services during the six weeks just prior to the Crusade than at any other time in the history of his ministry. He pointed out that this seemed to be a direct result of the extensive emphasis on witness, prayer, and evangelism that had preceded the actual Crusade meetings. A Presbyterian minister, in reporting the benefits of a Crusade to his congregation, noted, "A second specific result of the Crusade for our congregation has been a significant increase in worship attendance and in new members. This last fall we received ninety-two men and women into membership. This was the largest new members' class we have had in our church since 1920."

2. *To strengthen the church:* The second objective of Crusade evangelism is to strengthen the local church for witness and discipleship through renewal and training. Archbishop William Temple said, "The evangelization of those without cannot be separated from the rekindling of devotion of those within." Training, prayer, and an emphasis on witnessing result in a renewed and motivated congregation. This not only serves to reach the objectives of Crusade evangelism, but remains to serve the church under the leadership of the local pastor.

Among the affirming reports from local churches are the testimonies of two pastors which illustrate a Crusade's effectiveness in reaching this objective. A Lutheran pastor, reporting twenty-five additions to his church as a result of a Crusade, confirmed the efforts' effectiveness in evangelism. And he pointed out a second benefit, "More than this, the Crusade was a direct blessing to those who were already members. We did have countless individuals who, while they were members of the church, had little or no commitment to Christ. It was these people that the Crusade touched the most, and thus this became one of the most beneficial results of our participation." The pastor of the First Christian Church in Las Vegas wrote that within the three-year period from the time his church first began to prepare for a Crusade to the follow-through afterward, their stewardship increased 300 percent, their attendance 150 percent, and the number of first-time commitments to Christ 100 percent.

Prerequisites for Crusade Evangelism

There are certain prerequisites which need to be met before a city should enter into a Crusade. Three primary areas determine whether or not a city is prepared for multiple-church cooperative evangelism:

First, concern: There must be concerned, praying people who are burdened for lost mankind and who are depending on the power of the Holy Spirit to reach them. Jesus tells us, "The harvest truly is plenteous, but the laborers are few; Pray ye therefore the Lord of the harvest, that he will send forth laborers into his harvest" (Matthew 9:37–38, KJV). Over the years we have learned that a Crusade must be born out of a burden imparted by the Holy Spirit to local Christian leadership.

Often this begins with one or two persons. In Cincinnati, Ohio, one woman prayed for two years and then personally contacted ministers to interest them in a Crusade.

By the time the Crusade dates were established, she had departed to be with Christ, but her prayers and contacts resulted in more than 7,000 persons confessing Christ as Savior. At Anchorage, Alaska, two ministers prayed together weekly for six years about their city and state. In God's time, this resulted in a Crusade which trained hundreds of Christian workers in evangelism, affected Alaska's largest city, and spread the Gospel by television across the entire state. The Crusade meetings yielded a bountiful harvest of persons who acknowledged Christ as Savior and Lord.

One of the first steps in determining if it is God's will to hold a Crusade in your city is to see if the Spirit of God has communicated this concern throughout a cross-section of the Christian leadership of your area. A practical method for sampling that interest is provided. (See Appendix A—Steps for Developing a Crusade Invitation for Billy Graham Crusades, Step 1.)

Second, support: Adequate numbers of people from the involved churches are needed to make Crusade evangelism work. Personal evangelism requires only one Christian and one non-Christian; neighborhood evangelism involves a few persons; but city-wide evangelism, because of its sheer size and visibility, requires the involvement of much greater numbers. In choosing methods of moving dirt, it is important not to use a bulldozer to do what a single shovel can accomplish, and vice versa. Likewise, the appropriate method of evangelism must be chosen to fit the task.

Third, facilities: The practical factor of suitable meeting facilities of the right size which are available at the right time is necessary for optimum outreach in your community. Choosing the right-sized facility with good transportation access and adequate parking is important to accommodate your potential crowds. Too large a facility for what could reasonably be expected for attendance can discourage Christians and cause the work of evangelism to be discredited in the eyes of the public. Persons outside the church will judge the "success" of a Crusade by whether or not the stadium or auditorium was filled, rather than by the more appropriate standard of how well the potential for Crusade evangelism was realized in your community. Conversely, too small a facility can dim the vision and diminish the faith and commitment of involved churches and believers. A sense of vision is essential to inspire faith and evoke commitment. The ability to schedule these facilities at the ideal time for your target constituency is equally vital.

Ultimately Christian leadership in a community must answer this critical question: "Is it God's will that a Crusade be held in our city at this time?" A serious and prayerful evaluation of these three prerequisites in the order presented will help in answering that question. A first and practical step in exploring the interest and concern for a Crusade is to form an ad hoc or temporary committee which is representative of the Christian leadership of the metropolitan area. This committee should include about fifteen persons—men and women, clergy and laity—who have a concern for evangelism and a commitment to a Billy Graham type of Crusade. Committee members, representing the Christian life of the area, would give leadership to a continuing prayerful and practical process of exploration in future weeks and months. (See Appendix A—Step 2.)

Process: Laying the Foundation

As the ad hoc committee undertakes the vital function of determining if it is God's will for a Billy Graham Crusade to take place in their community at the present or some future time, two concepts about Crusade evangelism should be kept clearly in focus:

First, a Crusade must be built on biblical principles, not around a public personality. Some people welcome the public notoriety of a well-known evangelist like Billy Graham, feeling that this will ensure successful evangelism. Others criticize Crusade evangelism on this same basis, claiming that it fosters a personality cult. If the evangelist is carefully chosen and his motive is to exalt Christ, there is no reason why the New Testament pattern cannot be repeated, "And the two disciples heard him [John] speak, and they followed Jesus" (John 1:37, KJV).

Although it is helpful when inviting others to have a highly visible and popular person such as Billy Graham as the evangelist, he would never consider going to a city without certain principles being applied in the preparation process. Mr. Graham and his Team recognize that these biblical principles are essential to effective evangelism and discipleship. A discussion of these is given in Chapter Three.

Second, a Crusade is centered in the local church. Professor of evangelism, Lewis Drummond, has said, "God is on a mission of world redemption. And his basic plan for world evangelization is the use of the instrumentality of the church."[4] George Peters emphasizes that "as the Gospel [evangel] is central in the New Testament message, so must evangelism be central in the function of the church. According to the New Testament, the church lives by evangelism and for evangelism."[5] The Church, and specifically the local church, is God's agency for evangelism, nurture, discipling, worship, and service. As such, any evangelism effort should cooperate with, and be an extension of, the witness of the local church.

God has given gifts to the church, including the gift of an evangelist, and these gifts are most effective when exercised together. For the evangelist to "reap," the church must have already "sown." And in order to "make disciples," the fruit of the harvest must be related back to local churches. Churches function individually in sowing, come together corporately for proclamation, and then minister as individual local bodies in the follow-up process. The greater the number and scope of churches involved in preparation, and the greater the number of church members assuming some role of participation, the larger will be the impact on the total life of the community, as well as in each involved church.

In light of these concepts, the temporary committee then ascertains the extent of church support across their metropolitan area, encouraging the broadest possible church involvement. To sample further the interest of the Christian community, an Invitation Committee of 50 to 100 persons composed of clergy and lay leadership should be formed. In addition, letters of support from leaders in the Christian community and the community at large should be solicited. This will permit an objective look at the scope and depth of support, giving a sense of what the Holy Spirit has already done to prepare the hearts and minds of Christian leaders in the metropolitan area under consideration. (See Appendix A—Steps 3 and 4.)

Several factors need to be kept in view when developing an Invitation Committee. In the effort to touch the broader life of the community, it is important that as many churches as possible be involved in the invitation process before any Crusade plans are made. This will avoid the criticism that decisions were made first, and then churches were asked to take part in supporting "someone else's program." Some churches will be deeply committed to both the Crusade's methods and message. Others will support its message but have reservations about the methods, particularly regarding the extent of cooperation. Still others may have reservations about the emphasis of the message but not be troubled by the methods. The implications of participation in a Crusade are discussed in Chapter Five.

Third, it is important to provide acceptable opportunities for a broad spectrum of churches to become involved. This can be likened to concentric circles of persons standing around a fire. Some will stand close to it because they welcome both the heat and the light. Others will choose to be in one of the outer rings and experience only a portion of its warmth and illumination. (In time the warmth and light of the fire may draw them closer.) At this early stage, the circles should be kept broad enough so that as many churches as possible can comfortably identify with the prospect of a Crusade (see Figure 1). Ultimately, churches will be asked to make a much stronger commitment, but that will come after they have received additional information.

Figure 1.

At this stage in the invitation process, it is not recommended that the temporary committee ask for a vote of support by individual church bodies, denominational bodies, councils of churches, evangelical groups, or other organizations. Experience has shown that it is easy for one or two vocal persons to bring about a "no" vote in a large group, which then inhibits others who might wish to participate in a Crusade. On the other hand, even if the group votes unanimously for a Crusade, it does not guarantee that individual churches will become involved. This is a decision which must be made by each church, led by its pastor. Approaching the local pastor individually to determine his interest in involving his congregation in a potential Crusade has proven to be the most accurate and effective means of determining interest.

At this point of exploration and planning, a pastor or a congregation should never be placed in the position of saying an irreversible "no" to the Crusade. Given time and more information, they may choose to become involved, albeit cautiously. The organizational steps of developing an Invitation Committee, and accumulating letters of support, provide a tangible way to test the interest in a city for a Billy Graham Crusade. Also, it develops that interest in a way that can be expressed meaningfully to members of the evangelistic Team.

Fourth, the most important step is prayer. A successful Crusade can come about only through the blessing of God. Billy Graham has often said that there are three important elements in a Crusade—prayer, prayer, and prayer. A Crusade needs to be born in prayer, bathed in prayer, and built on prayer. The Scripture reminds us, "Except the Lord build the house, they labor in vain that build it" (Psalm 127:1, KJV). If God does not bless in response to the prayers of His people, all human efforts will be fruitless. The greatest priority in exploring a potential Crusade is praying for God's leading and blessing, and encouraging others to commit themselves to prayer also.

In Review:

A clear definition of the purpose of Crusade evangelism and the process for assessing local church interest are essential.

1. *Purpose*—The biblical mandate for evangelism is found in the Great Commission (Matthew 28:19) which emphasizes the making of "disciples," not just "decisions." To fulfill that mandate, two primary objectives of Crusade evangelism are:

   a. To evangelize the community by using a variety of evangelism methods with primary emphases given to large evangelistic meetings.

   b. To strengthen the local church for continuing witness and discipleship through renewal and training.

2. *Process*—If it is God's will for a Crusade to take place, a cross section of concerned leadership from the Christian community is assessed to determine the depth of interest. Guidelines for that assessment are as follows:

   a. Crusades are based on biblical principles and not around a public "personality."

   b. Crusades are centered on the local church to ensure a broad impact in the community, as well as to gain lasting results for the kingdom.

   c. As many churches as possible are involved in the initial stages of the invitation process. A nonthreatening atmosphere is provided for churches and their leadership to step into a circle of support without requiring that they be equally committed to all aspects of the project. A vote of support is not requested if it is not essential, and an individual or congregation is given the choice of becoming involved later on in supporting a Crusade.

   d. Prayer is the first priority in evangelism. People, methods, and materials are instruments, and it is only through prayer that these instruments become effective by the empowering of the Holy Spirit.

3
Principles:
Keys to Effective
Crusade Evangelism

"I'm not interested," wrote a pastor in response to the Crusade opportunity in his city. He pointed out that he had taken part in a Crusade in another city and his church had not received any significant benefits. Although the great majority of churches in a community usually support a Crusade and speak positively of the benefits, occasionally a minister will voice a similar complaint. A careful review with the dissenting clergy of the extent of their church's involvement in the Crusade process invariably reveals that few if any of the essential principles of Crusade evangelism were implemented by their local congregation.

The first decision a pastor and his congregation makes when a Crusade comes to their city is whether or not to participate. But a positive decision alone does not ensure that effective evangelism will occur or that the local congregation will benefit. Agreeing to the purpose of Crusade evangelism is not synonymous with involvement in the process. Commitment to a worthy goal is not enough. It must be pursued through methods that work.

Effective and enduring evangelism occurs when certain biblical principles are recognized and employed. This is especially true for Crusade evangelism where understanding and invoking these principles is vital both for the Crusade Team and for the sponsoring local churches. Local church leadership sometimes mistakenly assumes that Billy Graham and his Team will bring the Crusade with them like another piece of luggage. It can be neither packaged nor imported. Rather, successful Crusade evangelism results when the following key biblical principles are properly implemented.

Evangelism Is the Work of the Holy Spirit

First, evangelism is the work of the Holy Spirit (Acts 1:8). Jesus said, "It is the spirit that quickeneth; the flesh profiteth nothing" (John 6:63, KJV). Effective Crusades are not built on persuasion, personality, or promotion. They are built by depending on the Holy Spirit to do a lasting work. It is important that both pastor and congregation realize that only the Holy Spirit is able to convict of sin, call to repentance and faith, and convert people to Christ (John 16:8). If we could organize or persuade people into the Kingdom, we could also organize and persuade them out again. This kind of evangelism would merely be human manipulation. The work of wooing and winning people to Christ is a work that only the Holy Spirit can accomplish.

There is a tendency to look upon the "past successes" of Billy Graham Crusades, and assume that Billy Graham and his Team bring with them some kind of "self-contained blessing" which can superimpose a successful Crusade on an area. This is not true. Experienced personnel and the materials of the Billy Graham Team are only instruments which must be energized by the Holy Spirit if they are to be effective. If our trust is in human resources alone, we will only reap that which is human. But if our trust is in God and His work, we will reap a rich spiritual harvest from the Holy Spirit.

Since evangelism is a work of the Holy Spirit, *prayer becomes our greatest priority.* The blessing of God on previous Billy Graham Crusades came in response to "effectual fervent prayer" (James 5:16, KJV). That same intensity in prayer is the key to God's blessing in your city. Armin R. Gesswein, who led the prayer emphasis in a number of Billy Graham's early Crusades, said, "Without doubt this is the master secret behind the Graham Crusades through the years; there is no other way to account for such a massive work of God. . . .

"Martin Luther battled his way through the Reformation by prayer and the Word of God. In his mighty nineteenth-century revivals Charles G. Finney unceasingly stressed the primacy of prayer. . . . A man of prayer himself, he would take a strong intercessor with him when he was invited to a city—a 'Father Nash' or an Abel Clary, someone who would not even show up at the meetings, but who would intercede for them by the hour in some secret place. In a new location Finney would invariably find out who was praying there. He would ask, 'Is anyone here hearing from heaven?' "[1]

Gesswein continued, "A. T. Pierson, a Bible teacher of the last century, once observed that 'no revival has ever come about but by united supplicatory praying, as in the Acts; and no revival has ever continued beyond that same kind of praying.' Dwight L. Moody remarked that 'every work of God can be traced to some kneeling form.' "[2] Prayer prepares our hearts. It prepares the hearts of others and it prepares the soil for the good seed. We must begin on our knees! This is a divine priority in the work of evangelism, and as we exercise it in Crusades, so shall we experience the blessing of God.

Billy Graham has said, "The secret of each Crusade has been the power of God's Spirit moving in answer to the prayers of His people. I have often said that the three most important things we can do for a Crusade are to pray, to pray, and to pray." This was well illustrated during the March, 1984, Alaska Crusade where Billy Graham was fighting a throat problem. On Thursday night, as he started to preach, his voice suddenly gave out. Many people began to pray earnestly. Without prior notice, Mr. Graham invited Associate Evangelist Ralph Bell to give a testimony, and then called on John Wesley White to preach the sermon. The words of both men were used of God. Billy Graham returned to the pulpit to give the invitation, barely squeaking out the words. He ended his instructions to the inquirers in a hoarse whisper. There was no dynamic voice, no persuasive personality, not even Billy Graham doing the preaching. And yet one of the largest responses of inquirers all week came that night. On the way out of the building a Team member said to Billy Graham, "The Lord received glory for Himself tonight." Mr. Graham's response was, "Yes, He did, and it shows where the real power comes from!"

Reaping Requires Sowing

Second, reaping requires sowing. This principle must be clearly understood for effective evangelism to occur. Paul said, "I planted the seed, Apollos watered it, but God made it grow" (1 Corinthians 3:6, NIV). One sows, another waters, and then God brings the increase. Sowing is indispensable in the preparations for evangelism if we expect to reap souls.

In the New Testament economy, the gift of an evangelist is effective only as other gifts of the church are exercised. Christians must sow the good seed of the Word of God through their witness and water it with their loving concern and prayers to prepare the harvest for the work of an evangelist. Mr. Graham has often pointed out that his Team is privileged to come to an area and reap where others have sown. There can be no reaping where there has been no sowing. The obstetrician, no matter how skilled, cannot deliver physical life if conception and gestation have not occurred. This is true also of spiritual life. We sow through our witness to bring about spiritual conception. We water by our love and prayers through a period of gestation, and then in God's time spiritual life is brought forth. The physical process cannot be shortened or bypassed if we want healthy physical life. The same is true if we want to see healthy spiritual life.

In the great wheat fields of America's Midwest farmers plant the seed and care for it during the growing season. When harvest time comes, they often contract harvesting crews to combine the wheat. It is important that these crews work quickly while the harvest is ripe, and work thoroughly so as not to waste the harvest. Harvesters cannot take credit for the crop, they can only do their part in reaping. But when the harvest is in, both the farmer and the harvester rejoice together.

This is true of the spiritual harvest. Billy Graham has emphasized that whenever there is a successful Crusade, it is because faithful Christians have prepared the harvest. A recent survey of Crusade inquirers revealed that 82 percent responded to the invitation on the first night that they attended a Crusade meeting. The spiritual sowing in their lives by Christians resulted in hearts prepared for reaping through exercise of the gift of an evangelist. In this way the church experiences the partnership that Jesus spoke about when He said, "He that reapeth . . . gathereth fruit unto life eternal: that both he that soweth and he that reapeth may rejoice together" (John 4:36, KJV).

This same principle applies in every aspect of Crusade preparations. Paul said, "Whatsoever a man soweth, that shall he also reap" (Galatians 6:7, KJV). Sowing is involved in all areas of the preparations: prayer, witness, publicity, arrangements, finances, recruitment, and training. It requires weeks and months to make proper physical and organizational preparations for the harvest. Using an iceberg to illustrate a Crusade puts these preparations into proper perspective (see Figure 1).

Approximately 10 percent of an iceberg appears

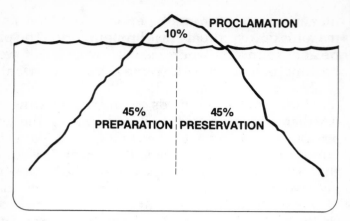

Figure 1.

above the surface of the water, and the 90 percent below is unseen. The visible part compares to the period when the Crusade meetings take place and publicity and advertising about the event pervades the community. Many people erroneously assume that this is all there is to an evangelistic Crusade. So often people are not aware of the tremendous amount of effort that goes into the preparation and the preservation which is essential to reaching the goal of "making disciples." Some have the mistaken notion that "a prayer, a poster, a preacher, and a place to meet" are all that is needed. Evangelists who have been involved in single-church or city-wide meetings preceded by limited preparations tell us the results are also very limited. There are no short cuts to preparing. That is why efforts are begun months in advance of the actual Crusade meetings in order to ensure a harvest.

Evangelism Is Built on Relationships

Third, effective evangelism is built on relationships. The earliest New Testament example of this is Andrew, who found his brother Simon and brought him to Jesus (John 1:40–42). This is a basic pattern for all evangelism. One person who has found new life, meaning, and forgiveness through an encounter with Jesus Christ is motivated by love to bring another to experience that same relationship with the Savior. As D. T. Niles has said, "Evangelism is one beggar telling another where he found bread." He is no better than his fellow beggar, but he is motivated by love to bring others to the "bread" that satisfies. This is what must happen in all evangelism methods, whether person to person or through small group Bible studies, Sunday school programs, worship services, visitation, single-church meetings, or city-wide Crusades.

Each Christian has a web of relationships in his life: family, friends, neighbors, fellow employees, students, casual acquaintances, and others. Church growth specialists have pointed out that the greatest outreach occurs through these relationships. Surveys of Crusade inquirers reveal that at least 80 percent of the unchurched who respond to the invitation were brought personally by someone else. Most Christians can point to a caring person who prayed for them. One survey of those who claim a personal relationship with Jesus Christ revealed that 85 percent could identify a relative within their family circle who had been praying for them. God has placed each Christian in the center of a web of relationships with persons to whom they can tell the good news (see Figure 2).

In recognition of this principle, some practical ways have been developed for Christians to identify and commit themselves to specific persons in their world of relationships. One program, titled Prayer Triplets, asks three Christians to each identify three persons in need of Christ and to meet weekly to pray together for these nine individuals. Another program, called Operation Andrew, is patterned after the example of Andrew in John 1:40–42. A simple card has been developed with one side providing a place for a Christian to list the names of seven persons who need Jesus Christ; and on the other side, five action steps are emphasized (see Figure 3).

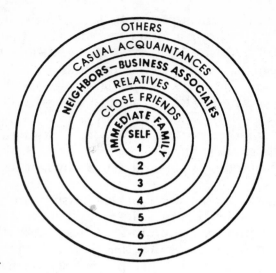

Figure 2.

The Prayer Triplet and Operation Andrew programs recognize that few of us are given the gift of an evangelist. From his studies Peter Wagner estimates that "in the average evangelical church 10 percent of the members have been given the gift of evangelist."[3] But all of us are given the privilege of being "light" and "salt" to the circle of relationships around us. Christians can effectively sow and water in the lives of others by loving acts which show they care. This makes the Christians' witness credible. Life-style evangelism proponent Dr. Joe Aldrich has said that people do not care to hear what we know, until they know we care. The success of evangelism begins at the level of personal loving and caring, and this is something that every true believer can do. The 90 percent of the congregation who prepare for the harvest are just as important as the 10 percent who have been gifted in harvesting.

The Operation Andrew concept also recognizes that cultivating the soil is essential before the seed is planted. Every farmer knows this and deals with the soil according to the condition in which he finds it. Some soil re-

Figure 3.

quires only light tilling, whereas other soil must be worked extensively with both plows and harrows to make it ready for the precious seed. Jesus' parable of the sower in Matthew 13 dramatically points out this principle. In three of the four places where seed fell, the ground had not been properly prepared and the seed did not bring forth fruit. But when the seed fell on good soil, "it produced a crop—a hundred, sixty or thirty times what was sown" (Matthew 13:8, NIV). Christians who commit themselves to Operation Andrew engage in cultivating the soil of another person's life by breaking down barriers through acts of kindness and friendship.

When one shows a genuine concern for, and a sacrificial commitment to, the needs of another person, it will often open his heart so that the seed of the Gospel will find good ground and bring forth a harvest many-fold what was sown. The secret to the harvest in Crusade evangelism is tens of thousands of Christians committing themselves to the concepts embodied in the Prayer Triplet and Operation Andrew programs.

Involvement Produces Commitment

Fourth, involvement produces commitment. Management experts tell us that "involvement plus participation equals commitment." When you are involved in the process and participate in the decisions, you will be committed to the end goals. When a man agrees to serve as an usher in the Crusade, he makes a commitment which positively influences his praying, his priorities, his family, his friends and neighbors, and his attendance at the meetings. When a woman agrees to sing in the choir or open her home for prayer, it affects her prayer life, her priorities, her family, her friends and neighbors, and her attendance at the meetings.

One goal of Crusade preparations is to involve as many people as possible in advance of the meetings in at least one meaningful role. The participation of thousands of persons is needed for the choir, Christian Life and Witness training, neighborhood prayer groups, Operation Andrew, visitation, and ushering. Giving to the Crusade is another way to participate. Each gift, however small, represents involvement. Through these and other ways, thousands of persons can be involved before the actual Crusade meetings.

Around each involved person's life is a circle, or web, of relationships. The involved person has both contact with, and influence on, other persons. Multiplying the number of involved people multiplies the number of these relationships. The larger the inner circle of involved persons, the greater the outer circle of persons who will be influenced to attend the Crusade services. This involvement has a direct effect on Crusade attendance, the number of unchurched who are invited to the meetings, and the amount of prayer generated for spiritually needy individuals and for all aspects of Crusade preparations (see Figure 4).

To facilitate this involvement, all Crusade activity is organized down to the local church level. This requires extensive organization, communication and recruitment. Churches can most effectively involve the maximum number of persons from their congregation by organizing a Crusade congregational committee. The organizational process and its relationship to the local congregation is more fully explained in Chapter Six on Preparation. By choosing capable and committed leaders for this committee, a pastor can delegate the respon-

Influence Through Involvement

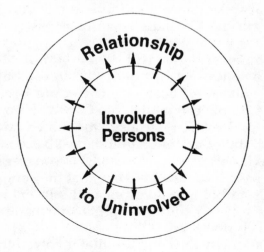

Figure 4.

sibility of involving his members, while personally encouraging the process publicly and guiding it privately in committee meetings. An approach that has helped other pastors become involved is for each pastor to think of the Crusade as though it were happening within the walls of his own church, and that his congregation is singly responsible for it.

The issue of involvement brings to a minister's mind relevant questions, "Why should I be involved? I'm already busy, and so are my people." "Won't this siphon off the energies of my people and slow down our own programs?" These legitimate questions are best answered by ministers who have become involved. The pastor of a 4,000-member Baptist church in Florida spoke to that question three years after a Crusade in his area. "To be a pastor is to have a full-time job no matter how big or little your church is. When something extra comes along like a Crusade, one has to think carefully whether or not the time is worth the investment. My view is that it's like sitting here hitting a spike with a tackhammer, and someone comes along with a sledgehammer. Well, Billy Graham comes along with a sledgehammer, and he hits that spike on the head in a tremendously effective way. So the Crusade is worth a pastor's investment."

Other ministers agree with this pastor. A Methodist pastor in a southwest city said, "We reaped a harvest from the Crusade because our people became involved." An Anglican minister in Canada reported that he had more than 150 referrals to his church (more than his usual Sunday morning attendance) before the Crusade ended, because he involved his congregation. A Lutheran pastor wrote, "I believe that the congregation which fails to become involved is the loser. We need some fresh winds of the Holy Spirit to move in our midst today. This is one avenue."

In city after city the churches that involved their people are the churches that later speak of the blessings from a Crusade. A survey of the 1976 Crusade in Seattle by Vanderbilt sociologist Glenn Firebaugh indicated that 80 percent of the ministers and 95 percent of the laymen involved in that Crusade felt that it had positive and lasting effects. The Scripture is true, "A man reaps what he sows" (Galatians 6:7, NIV). If we sow with the resources at our disposal—represented in the time and talents of the laity—God will return to us in full measure, pressed down and running over.

Every minister faces the question of priorities. He already has a full program with more than he can do. Involving his people by directing their time, energy, and abilities into a Crusade is an act of faith. It requires taking Jesus at His word when He says, "Give, and it shall be given unto you" (Luke 6:38, KJV). A Presbyterian minister from Florida commented on priorities in this way, "I would say to pastors to give the Crusade priority. That doesn't necessarily mean that the local church has to drop everything, and make the Crusade everything. I think the church's program is flexible enough that you can work it and make the Crusade top priority if you want to, and you stand to gain in every way from it." Ministers who have heartily involved themselves and their congregations have consistently reported that they have gained far more than they have given.

The minister of a Disciples of Christ church wrote, "One of the greatest dividends within the life of the church has been the growth of spiritual depth within the congregation. The number of Bible study and prayer groups has increased 500 percent. It must be said, however, that the blessings received by a church are commensurate with the level of participation. If a church's involvement is nominal, the results and blessings within that church will be limited. I heartily recommend the total and complete commitment and involvement of parish churches in the preparation, proclamation, and preservation surrounding the Crusade."

The pastor of a large and growing Baptist church was

in the midst of a major building program when the Crusade opportunity came to his city. After struggling with the problem of priorities, he chose to lead his congregation into deep Crusade involvement. When the Crusade was over, he offered these words of advice for other pastors who faced the opportunity of a Crusade. "Let me say, if I had a thousand tongues and could live a thousand lives, and if I had a thousand opportunities to do this all over again, I would do it! And if I could speak to every fellow pastor, I would say, 'If Billy Graham comes to your area, get into it early; get into it enthusiastically; get into it entirely; follow their game plan with prayer, and get ready for a blessing.' "

Organize for Effectiveness

Fifth, we must organize for effectiveness. Moses received good advice from his father-in-law, Jethro, who told him he was wearing himself out by seeking to judge all the people, and he should divide and delegate the responsibility (Exodus 18:13-26). That organizing is best accomplished by following the "3-D" Rule.

First, Divide into "Bite-Sized" Tasks—Moses used a one-to-five and one-to-ten ratio, asking one person to be responsible for the activities of five to ten others. The result was that he served the people and God's purposes far better than by trying to do it himself.

Second, Delegate the Responsibility—Good delegation occurs when we choose capable people who will commit themselves to a specific task that is equal to their talents. This requires defining the task and the responsibilities for that person, but it multiplies the leader's effectiveness and greatly increases involvement.

Third, Deadline its Completion—Whenever a specific task is given to a particular person, it is essential to specify when and how it must be completed. The assignment of realistic and meaningful time deadlines is imperative in reaching organizational goals.

Crusade evangelism seeks to implement this principle in order to mobilize the energies and abilities of the Christian community toward Crusade objectives with maximum effectiveness.

Establish Faith-Sized Goals

Sixth, faith-sized goals produce greater results. Establishing goals produces greater results since goals determine our priorities and priorities determine our schedule. It should be noted that "no goal" is also a goal and, if we aim at nothing, we are bound to hit it. It is essential, in a Christian context, to set goals too big to be reached by human resources alone, yet small enough so that you can believe—with God's help—they can be reached. Such goals need to be established prayerfully, with a realistic appraisal of the opportunities, the needs, and the resources . . . but always looking to God for His direction and assurance.

Goals should be established for every level of leadership. Major goals need to be set for the event itself, such as attendance, choir, ushers, counselors, and prayer involvement. Further, each local congregation involved in the event should be challenged to set goals for its own involvement, attendance, and giving. Church leaders are supplied with a goal-setting form that can be used to relate the opportunities of a Crusade to the local congregation. (See Appendix B: Goals for Action—Worksheet.)

Finally every person who becomes involved should be challenged to set goals in two ways:

First, by committing themselves to a place of service, such as a choir member, usher, counselor, prayer group leader, or visitation worker.

Second, each believer can be expected to be involved

in four general ways: by praying, by witnessing, by inviting others, and by attending.

Practical mechanisms should be provided to allow people to respond specifically in each of these areas, indicating their commitment to goals.

An Anglican minister converted in Billy Graham's 1954 London meetings and now a pastor in Edmonton, Alberta, wrote after the Crusade in that city, "I personally set a goal that every person in the congregation would be given an opportunity to attend at least one evening of the Crusade. That goal was almost realized, and we believe 85 percent of our congregation attended at least one meeting." He goes on to report that 65 members of the congregation made some commitment to Christ; and that another 60 persons, who had been prayed for and who had been brought to the meetings, were referred to his church. Seeking to involve every member of the congregation in some aspect of preparation will ensure the maximum spiritual return to the local congregation.

Train for Responsibilities

Seventh, train for responsibilities. Paul, in writing to Timothy, instructed him, "And the things you have heard me say in the presence of many witnesses entrust to reliable men who will also be qualified to teach others" (2 Timothy 2:2, NIV). Jethro admonished his son-in-law, Moses, to train the people in living so that his responsibilities of judging would be easier. He said, "Teach them the decrees and laws and show them the way to live and the duties they are to perform" (Exodus 18:20, NIV).

Each person recruited for involvement in an evangelistic event should be trained for his specific task and for the general responsibilities that every Christian should carry. That specific task might be leading a prayer group, serving as a counselor, working in follow-up, singing in the choir, helping as an usher, visiting others, or raising finances for the event. In addition, the training program should include both the challenge and the methods of sharing his/her faith, praying with others, and inviting others to the meetings.

Training is as essential in the preparation of an evangelistic event as it is in any other arena of life. It is unfair to assume people know how to do what they have never been trained to do. It is unrealistic to expect them to perform effectively without the resources of proper training.

Each of these seven principles needs to be applied as thoroughly as possible in preparing any evangelistic event and especially a Crusade. Specific programs for implementing these principles need to be tailored to the type of event, the resources available, the cultural context in which it is conducted, and other variables of your local situation. However, each principle should be considered indispensable for effective evangelism preparations.

Two Sides of Crusade Evangelism

Effective Crusade evangelism has two sides: a human side and a spiritual side. The key, humanly speaking, is involvement. The spiritual key is prayer. Someone has said action without prayer is arrogance, but prayer without action is hypocrisy. Both action and prayer are important. They must operate in the correct order and balance. Involvement is much like a scalpel in a surgeon's hand. It needs to be sharp, clean, and true, or else it will hinder the surgeon's work. But by itself, it is useless . . . only an instrument. The hand that holds the instrument is all-important. Through prayer we petition the Holy Spirit to use skillfully and powerfully the persons involved to bring about successful Crusade evangelism.

Down through the centuries Christian leaders have affirmed this balance between God's part and man's part. Martin Luther said, "It's not faith plus works, but faith that works." John Wesley called these two sides "man's best filled with the Spirit of God." William Carey expressed it this way, "We need to pray as though everything depended upon God, and work as though everything depended upon us."

In Review:

Understanding and applying the following principles are essential for effective Crusade evangelism:

1. Evangelism is a work of the Holy Spirit. Earnest prayer for the working of God's Spirit is the highest priority.
2. Reaping requires sowing. This is true of the spiritual harvest, and it is true of the organizational preparations.
3. Evangelism is built on relationships. Every Christian has a part in evangelism by his loving outreach to those who surround his life.
4. Involvement produces commitment. The larger the circle of involved people, the greater will be the surrounding circle of lives that are touched for evangelism.
5. Organize for effectiveness. Organizing the evangelistic event to divide, delegate, and deadline specific tasks will increase effectiveness.
6. Faith-sized goals lead to growth. The ultimate goal is that every member of the congregation be involved in some aspect of the Crusade ministry.
7. Train for responsibilities. Proper training of recruited personnel for both their specific task and general responsibility as a witness enhances performance.

4

Perspective:

Crusade Evangelism
and the Church

There is a Hindu fable of six blind men describing an elephant. The first blind man, touching the elephant's side, determined it was a wall; the second, clinging to the tusk, concluded it was a spear; the third, stroking the trunk, thought it was a huge snake; the fourth, holding a leg, concluded it was a tree; the fifth, clutching an ear, decided it was a fan; and the sixth, grasping the tail, was convinced he held a rope. Each man described the elephant from his limited perception; each lacked the ability to see the larger picture.

Understanding and applying the principles of Crusade evangelism also requires having the larger picture of the Church's mission in view. This is particularly important for the areas of: (1) evangelism and other ministries of the church; (2) Crusade evangelism and other forms of evangelism; and (3) Crusade evangelism and the local church. It will be helpful to consider each of these areas in perspective.

Evangelism and the Church

First, evangelism and other ministries of the church. Evangelism should be viewed neither as the only min-

istry of the church, nor as an optional, or even un-
essary, aspect of church life. In Ephesians 4 we read
that Christ, when He ascended, gave gifts or special
abilities to the church, "some to be apostles, some to
be prophets, some to be evangelists, and some to be
pastors and teachers, to prepare God's people for
works of service, so that the body of Christ may be
built up" (Ephesians 4:11–12, NIV). The gift of the
evangelist is certainly one of the major gifts given to
the church. Evangelism should be a top priority in the
ministry of the local church.

Emphasis on outreach is essential for the health
and life of the body. The Great Commission cannot
be fulfilled without the work of evangelism. Just as
the organs of our body are all essential for its health
and proper functioning, so each of the spiritual gifts
is important to the spiritual health of the church. One
gift cannot be eliminated and still maintain a healthy
body, especially a major gift. Dr. Louis Evans, Sr.,
former senior pastor of Hollywood Presbyterian
Church, has likened the ministry of the church to three
sides of a triangle: work, worship, and witness (see
Figure 1). You cannot take away one of the sides and
still retain the triangle's proper shape. Witness and

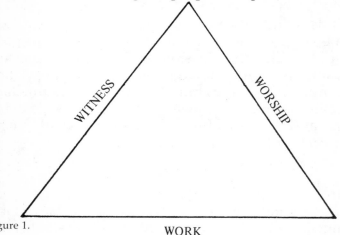

Figure 1.   WORK

evangelism are an essential ministry for wholeness in the church.

Peter Wagner, in emphasizing that evangelism has to be the top priority of a healthy church, notes: "A growth problem is bound to arise when the outreach priorities are switched. This has nothing to do with other kinds of priorities, such as commitment to Christ and commitment to the Body of Christ, both of which I believe need to precede outreach. But if a church that is otherwise in good health allows nominality to dim its belief that people without God have no hope, either in this world or in the world to come, and if the church does not act on this belief with aggressive evangelism, . . ." the church will enter a period of declining numerical growth.[1]

Emil Brunner has rightly said, "The church exists by mission as fire exists by burning." My observation of the thousands of churches across North America and other parts of the world (with which I have been privileged to work) is that growth stops when a clear sense of mission diminishes.

First, numerical growth declines and then spiritual life decays. Billy Graham has strongly affirmed this truth when he wrote, "Evangelism is the central mission of the church. Without it, believers become introspective and lacking in purpose, growth stagnates, worship becomes superficial, and selfishness stifles a spirit of giving." However, when a commitment to witness and evangelism is clearly a top priority for the local church, all other aspects of church life are enhanced as well.

Second, Crusade evangelism and other forms of evangelism. Billy Graham does not refer to his Crusades as "mass evangelism," although others have described them in that way. You cannot come to Christ "en masse." You must come individually. Dr. Leighton Ford has rightly stated, " 'Mass evangelism' is a platform for personal evangelism. It differs from the regular preaching of the Word of God in the church only in degree, not in kind.''[2] Billy Graham has often stated that mass evangelism is not necessarily the best form of evangelism. He believes the most effective form is personal evangelism. In essence, Billy Graham Crusades are designed to reap the efforts of personal evangelism in an aggregate setting. Christians sow and water, and God gives the increase as the gift of an evangelist is exercised.

Preaching to large crowds is only one of many evangelistic methods employed in Crusade evangelism. The preparations emphasize personal, small group, literature, radio, television, music, youth, and visitation evangelism, although these are not always readily seen by everyone. The highly visible part of Crusade evangelism admittedly is the time when thousands gather in a large auditorium or stadium; and hundreds, even thousands, respond to the call of Christ. The evangelism that takes place when large numbers come together during a Crusade is simply an extension of the same evangelism process that occurs in smaller numbers through individual contacts, families, neighborhood settings, and churches.

Although not the only method, nor always the ideal method, Crusades are a very effective way to evangelize when they are based and built upon the biblical principles which God has instituted and blessed down through the years. We should be careful not to set one method of evangelism against another. There are many effective methods and all are needed to reach every part of society. Paul said, "I have become all things to all men so that by all possible means I might save some" (1 Corinthians 9:22, NIV). The results of mass evangelism often encourage the start and continuation of many other forms of evangelism after Crusade meetings are over. The Right Reverend Maurice A. P. Wood, Bishop of Norwich, a participant in several Billy Graham Crusades, said, "I believe that mass evan-

gelism can be an immense encouragement to all forms
of personal witness, to sectional evangelism in schools
and colleges, and particularly in continuous local con-
gregation-based evangelism, using lay people in the
work."[3]

Crusades and the Local Church

Third, Crusade evangelism and the local church. Billy
Graham comes to a community only at the invitation
of the local churches. His gift is that of an evangelist
and, as with the other gifts given to the church, it
cannot be exercised effectively in isolation. The
church's gifts are inter-related and interdependent.
As Peter Wagner has said, "Church growth occurs
when the gift of an evangelist is being used, but it will
not happen if the other gifts are not operating simultaneously."[4] The evangelist exercises his gift in the
larger context of the Body of Christ across a whole city
or metropolitan area. It is the local church, however,
that prays for, prepares for, and preserves the results
of a Crusade. Since Billy Graham and his Team are
deeply committed to the local church, they will come
to an area only when the local Crusade organization
is broadly representative of the corporate life of concerned churches throughout that community.

A Crusade is not a substitute for any church's responsibility to evangelize. One giant event held every
ten to fifteen years will not compensate for a lack of
daily witnessing by the church. Neither will it infuse
complete spiritual health to a local body that has not
given emphasis to evangelism for years. It will help a
local congregation but it cannot restore it to full spiritual vitality—any more than a week's exercise can
restore to full health a body which has shunned physical activity for a decade. Rather, a Crusade is a sup-
plementary method to assist healthy churches who
are already doing evangelism. By uniting together in

this method, the combined resources of individual congregations can effectively witness to an entire area or community with an impact that could not be made when operating as separate local bodies.

A Crusade also becomes a source of renewal and reaping for congregations who have not usually been involved in evangelism. A Presbyterian minister, who had been converted thirty years earlier in one of Billy Graham's Crusades, wrote about the impact of the meetings in his community, "The months of preparation with congregations and visitation during the summer prior to the Crusade, plus the publicity and prayers during the Crusade, brought to thousands of people a new sensitivity to matters of the spirit. In our fast-paced, secularized, materialistic society, this powerful reminder of the spiritual dimension of life is something none of us pastors or laypeople in local congregations can accomplish on our own."

A city-wide Crusade should not be thought of as a single method but rather as a mission whose scope encompasses an entire city or metropolitan area, and which employs a variety of methods based on biblical principles. A Crusade is effective in serving the church when it is looked upon not as an isolated event or end in itself, but rather as part of a process of achieving larger long-term goals. The most effective Crusades occur when local Christian leaders have already demonstrated a concern for evangelism and renewal for their area and where their goals go far beyond an "event." In this context, a Crusade is effective as part of God's process for bringing about evangelism, renewal, and church growth.

In Review:

A proper perspective of Crusade evangelism reveals that:

1. Evangelism is complementary to the other minis-

tries of the church, not competitive with them. Each needs the other for the total health of the body, and for the fulfillment of the Great Commission.

2. In Crusade evangelism many different methods are emphasized. Mass evangelism is merely an extension of other forms of evangelism and, particularly, personal evangelism.

3. The evangelist comes to serve the corporate church across an entire metropolitan area through a city-wide Crusade. It is not a method, but rather a mission that uses a variety of evangelism methods based on biblical principles. It has long-term goals of evangelism and renewal for individual congregations and for an entire metropolitan area.

5
Participation:
Involving the Local Church

The local church pastor faces a choice . . . whether or not to participate in the Crusade! Participation offers a pastor and his church a challenging opportunity to declare Christ in an effective and powerful way across an entire city or region. But for some pastors it also raises significant questions such as: (1) "Can I support this expression of the Gospel?" (2) "Can I cooperate with the other churches that become involved?" and (3) "What will be the practical basis of cooperation?"

The ministry of some pastors has emphasized applying the Gospel to the social needs of hurting humanity, whereas the primary emphasis of a Crusade is the proclamation of the good news. These pastors may question whether or not they can commit themselves to Crusade objectives. Other clergy face a different question. Having sought diligently to maintain the integrity of their message and the purity of the church, they worry that their cooperation with others involved in the Crusade process will compromise their doctrinal position and the clarity of their witness. Still other pastors have practical questions about the basis of Crusade organization, finances, and follow-up. These are valid questions, and a decision about participation can best be made when these matters are brought into proper focus.

Proclamation Versus Application

For some pastors and their congregations the application of the Gospel to poverty, prejudice, and injustice in the community is a primary emphasis, while proclamation of the good news is a secondary. The opportunity to become involved in a project for proclamation raises certain concerns for them: "Will I be diverting my efforts?" "Will I be disowning my commitment to the social aspects of the Gospel?"

The choice between proclamation and application is not mutually exclusive. Senator Mark Hatfield, speaking at the U.S. Congress on Evangelism, called this distinction an "artificial polarization." The Billy Graham organization does not emphasize two distinct gospels, for the same God who created the soul and spirit also created the body. Certainly, the Gospel is intended to be "good news" to the *whole* person. Jesus Himself increased in wisdom (intellectually), in stature (physically), and in favor with God (spiritually) and man (socially) (Luke 2:52, KJV), to meet perfectly any need mankind would face.

The Gospel has many implications, and no one in a short period of time can preach all of them. When Billy Graham is invited to a community as the evangelist, his responsibility is to be a proclaimer of the good news as revealed in the Word of God, "how that Christ died for our sins according to the scriptures; And that he was buried, and that he rose again the third day according to the scriptures" (1 Corinthians 15:3–4, KJV). The evangelist takes this historic message and applies it to the needs, hurts, fears, frustrations, and sins of contemporary man. He will preach against sin on both an individual and a corporate basis.

Missiologist Dr. George Peters has said, "Crusade evangelism does not address itself *solely* to the individual and his sins and for salvation. It must become the voice of God to the people and nation, speaking boldly about the binding, blinding, and blighting sins of the nation, society, and institutions and calling all men to repentance."[1] Billy Graham points out the injustices and the inhumanity of man, emphasizing the need for Christians to be involved socially. But his primary emphasis in proclamation is to invite individuals to repentance and faith in Jesus Christ. This is the purpose of Crusade evangelism.

Mr. Graham has further set forth his convictions regarding the social implications of the Gospel in these words:

> "It is my conviction that even though evangelism is necessarily confined with narrow limits, the evangelist must not hedge on social issues. The cost of discipleship must be made plain from the platform. I have made the strongest possible statements on every social issue of our day. In addition, in our Crusades we have tried to set an example. Naturally there are some statements that I made a few years ago on sociopolitical affairs that I would like to retract. Yet I am more convinced than ever before that we must change men before we can change society. The international problems are only reflections of individual problems. Sin is sin, be it personal or social, and the word 'repent' is inseparably bound up with 'evangelism.' Social sins, after all, are merely a large-scale projection of individual sins and need to be repented of by the offending segment of society."[2]

Pastors and congregations do not have to abdicate their commitment to the social aspects of the Gospel in order to participate in a Crusade. In fact, as we will see in later chapters, they may actually enhance it. The issue is one of proper sequence. In addressing the European Congress on Evangelism Billy Graham said, "I do not believe there are two gospels: a social gospel and a redemptive gospel. There is only one Gospel! But too many of us have put the cart before the horse. It was not by accident that the first four of the Ten Commandments deal with man's relationship to God, and the last six deal with man's relationship to his neighbor. Zacchaeus gave back fourfold . . . but only after Jesus went home with him. He would not have given 400 percent in restitution, had he not had an encounter with Jesus first."[3]

In every Crusade scores of people with a new or renewed commitment to Christ are motivated by the love of Christ to reach out and meet the needs of their fellow man. In fact, Mr. Graham's instruction to those who respond in his meetings often include statements such as: "Go out of your way to befriend someone of another race"; "Witness by showing love to your neighbor"; and, "Invite someone of another ethnic background to your home for dinner."

Cooperating With Others

For other pastors and their congregations participation in a Crusade raises the question of cooperation and association with persons and churches holding different theological views from their own. I recall addressing a group of clergy in Canada where the question was asked, "How do you decide which churches should be allowed to participate in a Crusade?" The intent behind that question is really a prior question which could be expressed this way, "How do you maintain the purity of the church in an inter-church cooperative ministry?" The fear is that persons who hold theological views that differ from their own may negatively infect them with a different theology or cloud the clarity of their witness. These legitimate concerns can best be dealt with by clarifying the real choice involved.

Involvement in a cooperative evangelistic effort does not imply total agreement by all parties in all matters. It does not mean that everybody involved totally agrees theologically with everybody else. One church may require many gallons of water for baptism, while another church needs only a cup. Cooperation also does not mean that everybody involved is in total agreement with all methodology. Some churches rarely or never give a public invitation, while others extend one every Sunday. Many clergy look on an area-wide Crusade effort in a different light from their local church practices. As one minister said, "We do not usually use this method in our church, but I see value in it for a city-wide effort." Finally, cooperative evangelism does not mean that those churches who become involved across denominational lines are changing their theological position or compromising their doctrinal distinctives.

Cooperative evangelism means that those who become involved have a common desire to give witness to Jesus Christ throughout a whole community or area. Their willingness to become involved is usually born out of common agreement on the message of the Gospel, and a conviction that there are times and ways and places where "the Church" can accomplish its work better cooperatively than it can individually. It also means that those who become involved believe they can commit themselves to this project at this time. There will be other projects for church growth, social action and family life, which they may also choose to have a part in at some future time. These are not mutually exclusive decisions.

Cooperative evangelism is not union. It does not require congregations to make a long-term organizational commitment to one another. The organization for a Crusade ceases when the project is complete. Cooperative evangelism is not uniformity. It does not require everyone to be pressed into the same theological, methodological, or ecclesiastical mold. Rather, it shows a unity of purpose. It is the common desire to make known to the whole community Jesus Christ as

Savior and Lord; and to call men and women of all ages to a commitment to Him. This kind of unity causes us to subordinate our differences, and affirm the things that unite us in order to lift up Jesus Christ. In essence, churches that come together in Crusade evangelism practice the principle espoused by an earlier Christian leader who said, "In essentials, unity; in incidentals, diversity; and in all things, charity."

In the issue of maintaining the church's purity, the crucial question is, "Who is being influenced?" The Scriptures assure us that the Gospel "is the power of God unto salvation to every one that believeth" (Romans 1:16, KJV) and "the word of God is quick, and powerful, and sharper than any twoedged sword" (Hebrews 4:12, KJV). In a Billy Graham Crusade it is this Gospel, based on the Word of God, that will be preached in the power of the Holy Spirit. The promises of Scripture assure us that this message will influence positively those who are exposed to it through their involvement. The biblical integrity of the messenger, the message, the methods, and the materials are a known fact in a Billy Graham Crusade.

How Do You Decide?

Then how does one decide which churches will have a part in a Crusade? The best method of deciding is one that Jesus used: when Jesus invited men and women to follow Him, He did not give them a theological examination. Rather, He clearly spelled out the demands of discipleship and the result was that "from that time many of his disciples went back, and walked no more with him" (John 6:66, KJV). They sorted out themselves based on the commitment required.

Neither the local committee nor the Billy Graham Team decides which churches may participate. It is not possible for the Graham organization, or even the local committee, to determine which denominations and churches should be involved in a Crusade and which should not. The theological commitments of pastors within a particular denomination will vary from city to city and within a given city. The best method for selecting those who participate in a Crusade is to identify clearly the requirements of participation and let each local pastor and congregation decide if they can and will meet these requirements.

Writing on the subject of cooperative evangelism, Dr. Robert Ferm has pointed out, "The cooperative policy of evangelism leaves the door open for the entrance of any and all who desire to have the Gospel preached with unparalleled effectiveness. Every true Christian has a great responsibility for being identified with the work of God. The words of Jesus are perennially true, 'He that gathereth not, scattereth.' "[4]

What Are You Committing To?

The issue facing a pastor or congregation is not whether they can commit themselves to other congregations, but whether they can commit themselves to the purposes and programs of Crusade evangelism. When Billy Graham comes to a community, it is clearly known that he comes to preach the Gospel from the Scriptures. He invites men, women, and young people to make a personal commitment to Jesus Christ. Those who respond are counseled by trained counselors who have met specific qualifications. These inquirers are given Bible study materials and related back to local churches for follow-up and nurture. It is about this project, for this purpose, that congregations must choose. The pastor then makes his own choice as to whether or not he leads his congregation to involvement, and the degree of that involvement.

Dr. Ferm has further emphasized the importance of love and unity within the church as a witness to the unbelieving world. "Therefore, in a period of unprecedented opportunity for spreading the Gospel to the ends of the earth, there is not time for needless exposure of differences of opinion but a necessity for Christian love that will enable all true servants of Christ to work together for world evangelism. 'Love one another with a pure heart fervently,' is the command of the Scriptures. 'By this shall all men know that ye are my disciples, if ye have love one toward another.' These are the words of the Savior whose evangel is being proclaimed. How much greater would be the impact today if every professing Christian would unite in a major offensive invading enemy territory in a spiritual war of aggression! How much more glorifying to Christ would the entire work of evangelism be if the unbelieving world would be confronted with a Church united for evangelism!"[5]

Fire, Not Fences

Over the years it has been made clear that the best way to maintain the purity of the church is not through the fences of separation, but through fire: the fire of the Holy Spirit. Fences are effective only in separating people, but the Holy Spirit is a refining fire who can purify individuals and renew churches. As Christians pray, all aspects of a Crusade should be so filled with the Holy Spirit that those who become involved will find the "fire" a purifying and refining influence in their own lives.

Integrity Is Essential

Although participation in cooperative evangelism presents some pastors and congregations with questions of either application or association, the most important issue is trust. Pastors who lead their people to become involved with other congregations and with the Crusade Team must have confidence in the Crusade organization. There must be confidence in the integrity of the individuals who make up the evangelistic Team, the message that is proclaimed, the methods that are implemented, and the materials that are used. In addressing evangelists at Amsterdam 83 Billy Graham strongly affirmed this principle by exhorting them to "communicate the Gospel by living a holy life. Our world today is looking for men and women of integrity. We must have communicators who back up their ministry with their lives."[6] A series of affirmations adopted at that Conference represent a biblical standard for responsible evangelism today. (See Appendix C: The Amsterdam Affirmations.)

In order to maintain integrity, policies have to be established that are fair to all involved, clearly understood, and enforceable. As a result of years of Crusade experience, the Billy Graham Association has identified three primary areas of policy which are explained to a local committee when a Crusade invitation is accepted. These areas include Crusade organization, Crusade finances, and follow-up referrals.

First, Crusade organization. A Crusade is a local effort and should be guided by an Executive Committee composed of laymen and clergy who are representative of the local Christian community. It is important that every principal Christian group in the area be involved in the planning, and suitably represented on the Executive Committee. This committee will become incorporated under the laws of the state or province and will be responsible for the policies, outreach, and results of the Crusade. The Billy Graham Association will serve in an advisory capacity to the Executive Committee, sharing personnel, methods, materials, and other resources to assist them in reaching the Crusade goals. The local Crusade corporation will be dissolved within six months following the completion of the Crusade meetings—in order to avoid its use for any purpose other than that for which it was specifically established. It is a matter of trust for those who commit themselves to this project that the Crusade organization will not be utilized for other purposes in the future. (See Appendix D: Basic Concepts of Crusade Organization.)

Second, Crusade finances. The reputation of evangelism, like many other enterprises, has been hurt by inadequately managed financial procedures, and sometimes by outright dishonesty. It is absolutely essential that the churches and the public at large know that Crusade funds are being handled in a manner that commands respect and shows genuine integrity. The handling of Crusade finances should be a credit to the witness to Christ and the work of evangelism in the community.

To be sure that all Crusade finances are handled with the highest level of integrity, we established the following policy:

A. *Budget*—The Crusade budget is established by the local Executive Committee with advisory help from the BGEA Team. That committee will receive, account for, and disburse all funds.

B. *Accounting*—The local Crusade Office will issue tax-deductible receipts for all gifts. At the end of the Crusade an audit will be prepared by a public accountant and published in the newspapers, as well as sent to participating churches.

C. *Team Expense*—The evangelist comes at no salary expense to the local Crusade. His salary is paid out of the Minneapolis office and he receives no personal remuneration from the local committee. Billy Graham has not accepted as personal remuneration a love gift, an offering, or an honorarium since 1952 when he went on annual salary. This is done to avoid the implication that the evangelist is coming for his own personal enrichment. Prorated salaries and expenses for other Team members will be placed in the Crusade budget with prior agreement by the Executive Committee.

D. *Fund Raising*—Funds are raised primarily on a personal solicitation basis. Churches are not assessed. That is, they are not assigned a certain amount of money per person as a quota. However, it is hoped that every church will voluntarily become involved financially for its own spiritual profit, and in order to share the financial responsibility across a broad base. Usually more than half of the Crusade budget is raised in advance of the meetings, so that undue emphasis on funds will not be made in Crusade offering appeals.

Third, follow-up referrals. Since the purpose of Crusade evangelism is to "make disciples," it is imperative that the inquirers who respond in the meetings be related to local churches for follow-up and spiritual nurture. This goal must be achieved in a way that is fair to the local churches of the area and is helpful to the inquirer's spiritual growth. Policy specifics and the priorities that shape them are covered in the chapter on Preservation.

A Response to Integrity

A minister from a mainline denomination reflected on his experience in a Billy Graham Crusade. "I'll have to admit that I entered into the Crusade planning some months ago with some fear and trepidation. Oh, I have always respected Billy Graham deeply and have been impressed by his integrity and special gift of communication. But, because of my own rigid, legalistic, and separatistic Christian background, I was afraid that there might be a lot of cliché-ridden emotional coercion, manipulation, and 'laying on' of false guilt.

"All my anxieties were for naught. The Crusade week was one of the most beautiful experiences of my life, and a tremendous climax to a year of the most thorough and conscientious preparation I've ever seen for any event. The amount of quality effort put into preparing counselors and churches for follow-up is nothing short of super-human (Holy Spirit miraculous I'd say!). And that quality effort and the excellent materials that go along with it (not grinding any theological ax) is another sign of integrity. I don't know of any other evangelistic organization that does it so conscientiously. They do it because it's the responsible thing to do, and they do it well!''

The Pastor Is the Key

Once a pastor determines that the basis of participation in a Crusade is both acceptable and desirable, he faces a second question as to how deeply he will involve his church. The key to effective and extensive involvement by the local congregation is the pastor. Alfred Sloan's definition of an organization as "the lengthened shadow of a man" reinforces the fact that a pastor is key to his church's priorities. This is echoed by Dr. C. B. Hogue, former secretary of evangelism for the Southern Baptist denomination:

"The most influential voice in the life of the church comes from the pulpit. Several times each week the pastor has an opportunity to share his vision of the church and its mission. If he speaks with God-given assurance and urgency, the pastor can, through his weekly sermons, motivate, encourage, challenge, inspire, and infect his people with his insights into the good news."[7]

The pastor influences his people not only by exhortation, but also by example. This truth is affirmed by Faris Daniel Whitesell, who has said, "The pastor must lead his people in intercessory prayer for the lost; he must inspire them, teach them, organize them, send them out, and encourage them to continue in this greatest of all church work."[8] Evangelism professor C. E. Autry further echoes this theme, "The place of the pastor in the evangelism [growth] of the local church is strategic. . . . The degree to which the pastor is evangelistic will be reflected in the church. If he is lukewarm, the church will very likely be likewise. If he is intensely evangelistic, the church will reflect the warmth and concern of the pastor."[9]

The Crusade staff can provide the methods, but the motivation to implement them within the local church must come from the local pastor. Like a car without gasoline, the ministry won't go far without proper motivation. Methods will work only if there is a commitment by the pastoral leadership to use these methods with energy and enthusiasm. That commitment is essential, for it will signal to the congregation what their degree of commitment should be.

Paul reminded us that "whatsoever ye do, do it heartily, as to the Lord, and not unto men" (Colossians 3:23, KJV). The pastor who treats a Crusade as though it is "someone else's priority," which he merely accommodates in the church calendar and his personal calendar, will see limited benefits to his church. In order for a local church to benefit from this opportunity, the pastor needs to own it as though it were his own idea, and involve his congregation as though each member is solely responsible for making the Crusade happen. For truly, you will reap what you sow.

In Review:

Participation in a Crusade occurs with the following understanding:
1. The local committee does not decide which churches may participate. Rather, individual churches decide for themselves—based on the purposes and programs of a Crusade. This is Jesus'

principle of letting His followers choose, based on the cost of following Him.

2. Cooperative evangelism is not a horizontal union requiring uniformity among all participants. It is a vertical unity whereby we commit ourselves to a common purpose, the proclamation of the Gospel.

3. The purity of the church is best maintained by the "fire" of the Holy Spirit rather than the "fences" of human separation.

4. To maintain the integrity of Crusade evangelism, policies must be fair, clearly understood, and enforceable—especially in the areas of organization, finance, and follow-up.

5. The local pastor is the key to involving his congregation.

6
Preparation:
The Organizational Process

Identifying principles can be like speaking in parables. The truth is best understood when applied. Biblical principles for evangelism, and in particular Crusade evangelism, are best illustrated through their application. Although it is not our intention here to provide detailed procedures in Crusade preparation, a broad overview of the preparation process will help illustrate for the reader the principles outlined in previous chapters.

Four Phases of the Crusade Process

The principles involved in Crusade evangelism are "fleshed out" in four general phases of activity: organization, recruitment, training, and function. These activities are essential in any evangelism project. A review of these phases and the Crusade development sequence will help local church leadership to understand and relate effectively to the schedule of preparation activities. (See Appendix E—Sample Crusade Involvement Schedule.)

1. *Organization:* The organization phase involves a development of lines of responsibility and communication from the Crusade Executive Committee down to each local church. Generally, this is accomplished by a mobilizing structure for three

committees: Ministers, Congregational Leaders, and Youth (see Figure 1). This phase begins with the formation of the Executive Committee and ends with the establishment of a Crusade congregational committee in each participating church (see Figure 2). Usually this occurs in the first three or four months of Crusade preparations (see Figure 3).

2. *Recruitment:* The purpose of the recruitment phase is to commit thousands of local church members to serve in some area of the Crusade outreach ministry: choir, ushers, counselors, prayer groups, laymen's committee, women's committee, Operation Andrew, finance, visitation, and youth. The re-

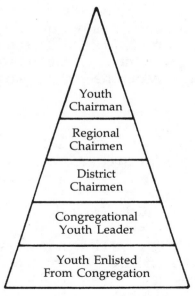

Figure 1.
Three primary mobilizing committees in Crusade preparations organize the total Crusade area into regions and districts in order to keep a "leadership-to-contact" ratio of one to ten or less. The committees are: Ministers, Congregational Leaders, and Youth. Using the Youth Committee as an example, the pyramid of organization is pictured above.

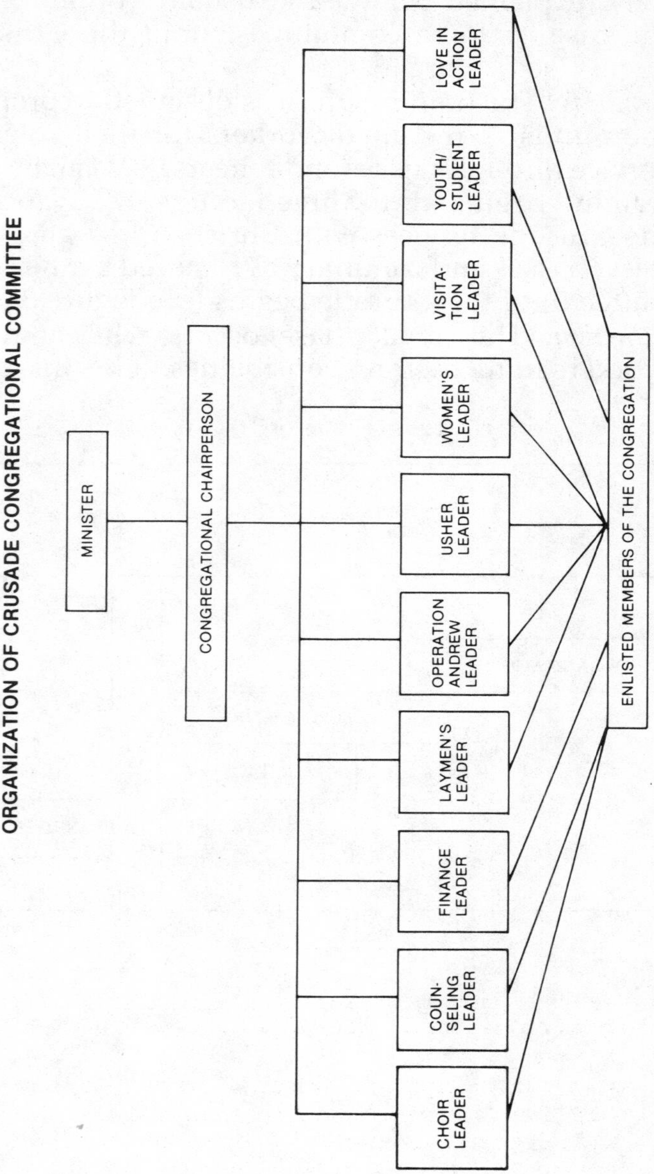
ORGANIZATION OF CRUSADE CONGREGATIONAL COMMITTEE
MINISTER
CONGREGATIONAL CHAIRPERSON
CHOIR LEADER
COUN-SELING LEADER
FINANCE LEADER
LAYMEN'S LEADER
OPERATION ANDREW LEADER
USHER LEADER
WOMEN'S LEADER
VISITA-TION LEADER
YOUTH/ STUDENT LEADER
LOVE IN ACTION LEADER
ENLISTED MEMBERS OF THE CONGREGATION

Figure 2.

cruitment effort is launched at the church leaders' rally (explained below) and usually continues, in the case of some committees, until the Crusade begins (see Figure 3).

3. *Training:* The training phase is designed to prepare thousands of recruited workers for their roles of service through classes and rehearsals. Usually this training begins up to three months in advance of the Crusade services with Christian Life and Witness Classes and continues as required by the committee until the Crusade begins (see Figure 3).

4. *Function:* This final phase occurs when trained workers fulfill their responsibilities. It begins up to

PHASES OF CRUSADE ORGANIZATION

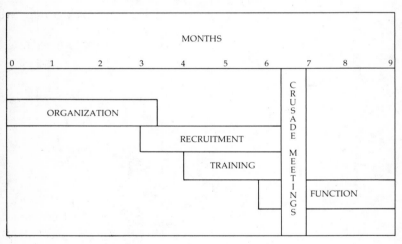

Figure 3.

one month in advance of the Crusade services with the start of the home prayer program, and continues for months afterward during the follow-up activities. Generally speaking, most workers perform their tasks during the Crusade period itself (see Figure 3).

Every Crusade committee which recruits involvement from the local congregation goes through these four phases. The cycle may overlap for different committees, depending on when they fulfill their particular functions.

Church Leaders' Rally

The Church Leaders' Rally, which completes the organizational phase of Crusade preparations and launches the recruitment phase, is an important event in the preparation process. Usually three to four months in advance of the Crusade services, all pastors, staff, and leaders recruited to serve on local church committees, along with their spouses, are invited to this rally for inspiration and instruction. At this time many of the principles outlined in the *previous* chapters are put into practice in a specific way.

Inspiration is the main emphasis during the first hour of each rally. This is often provided through the participation of Crusade musicians, such as George Beverly Shea, Myrtle Hall, John Innes, and/or Tedd Smith, with a message by Cliff Barrows. Best known for his platform work and the leading of the choir in large Crusade meetings, Mr. Barrows is equally effective as a preacher. He has a warm and personal style of communication. His enthusiasm and integrity of life builds confidence in, and commitment to, Crusade goals.

Instruction is the emphasis of the second hour of the rally. Leaders are divided into groups according to their area of responsibility. Each of these groups is given an overview of its task and shown how this breaks down into various phases and steps. The first step is defined for them with a deadline for completion—important in achieving any goal. Each church leader is asked to set goals for his task and is given a date for reporting the fulfillment of those goals. In addition to fulfilling his specific committee requirements, each leader is requested to pray regularly for the Crusade preparations and for persons in need of Christ. He should begin to generate interest in the Crusade by talking to friends and neighbors and inviting them to the meetings.

Pastors and congregational leaders who comprise one of the groups receive an overview of the Crusade development schedule for the weeks ahead, plus a brief description of the responsibilities outlined for each of the local church leaders. They are urged to complete the recruitment of their congregational committees, if this has not already been done, and to assist and encourage their leaders in fulfilling assignments received at the rally. The importance and benefits of involvement are emphasized, pointing out that the forming of a Crusade congregational committee makes the task of involving a maximum number of members in each congregation manageable. Congregational leaders and pastors should meet with their full committee at least once each month for coordination, encouragement, and prayer.

Other church leaders receive instruction as follows:
1. *Choir:* Choir leaders are challenged to recruit several thousand persons for a large Crusade choir. The choir not only provides a musical ministry to enhance the services—allowing people to use their talents to the glory of God—but also provides a wonderful opportunity to bring persons under the preaching of the Gospel who might not usually come to the services. Local churches often discover that a member of the congregation who will not

commit himself to a regular church choir will become involved in an effort that lasts for only one week. The blessing of this experience often motivates them to volunteer for their own church choir following the Crusade. One minister reported that his church choir had new enthusiasm and their numbers increased by 50 percent following a Crusade in his city.

2. *Counseling and Follow-Up:* Counseling and follow-up leaders are challenged to recruit persons for the Christian Life and Witness Classes which prepare people for personal evangelism, discipleship, and to serve as counselors during the Crusade. These classes, taught by BGEA personnel, also equip counselors to do personal follow-up after the Crusade is over.

   Ministers frequently speak of the benefits that these classes bring to their congregation following a Crusade. A Lutheran pastor who urged his members to attend the classes saw 400 participate—more than in any other program he had offered his church. After the Crusade he had more volunteers to teach Sunday school than he had classes available. A Presbyterian minister wrote, "One of the special impacts of the Crusade for our congregation was in the area of training for evangelism among our leaders. The classes on 'Christian Life and Witness' held in our sanctuary provided invaluable orientation to over 150 men, women, and teenagers of our congregation for their personal witnessing. Beyond the practical assistance in sharing their faith with others, these classes gave new confidence to the ones I spoke with regarding the clarity and strength of their own relationship to Christ."

3. *Finance:* Each participating church is invited to appoint a finance leader. At the meeting of these leaders the Crusade budget, financial policy, and fund-

raising strategy are reviewed. Although local churches are not required to make a budget commitment, each church is encouraged to become involved financially for its own spiritual benefit and to spread this responsibility over the broadest possible base. Finance leaders are asked to consult with their pastor and official boards concerning the establishment of a "faith-sized" financial goal, and then choose a method for reaching that goal which best suits their congregation.

In one city a Baptist pastor reported that his local church's finance campaign conducted several weeks after the Crusade exceeded its goal by $100,000. He explained that he did not have a large increase in members, but the existing congregation had a new priority for their dollars and a new commitment to the work of Christ. An Anglican pastor, following a Crusade, wrote, "Our offerings have increased between 20 and 25 percent since the Crusade. We certainly did not do our planning for this, but God is wonderful in His blessing to us. It is fairly obvious that when Christians become more committed to Christ, their gifts to the Lord's work also increase."

4. *Laymen:* Lay leaders are asked to encourage men to participate in every area of the Crusade and, in particular, to involve them in prayer and in small group Bible studies known as nurture groups. The leaders are challenged to multiply their numbers in the congregation and to organize interdenominational prayer meetings at their place of work. A Crusade offers an excellent vehicle for involving and mobilizing more laymen in the church.

The training and renewing from these opportunities has a positive influence on the spiritual life of the church. A Canadian pastor wrote, "We have found that the more you get involved, particularly in the areas of . . . [Bible] studies and enthusiastically building in preparation for the Crusade, then the more results you will see in the marvelous and wonderful things happening in personal lives and in the life of the church. We believe this church under God will never be the same! The congregation has grown spiritually and in numbers, and is still continuing to grow. There is an even deeper awareness of our responsibility to evangelize, and we are continuing to train others in this ministry."

5. *Operation Andrew:* Operation Andrew (OA) leaders are urged to promote the OA emphasis in their congregation through two primary emphases:

   a. Challenging members to fill out an Operation Andrew card, to commit themselves to pray for up to seven people and to seek to bring them to the services;

   b. Planning delegations of men, women, and young people to the Crusade and providing transportation with church buses.

   Each leader is urged to meet with his pastor and establish an Operation Andrew Sunday when the minister will preach a sermon on this emphasis and distribute Operation Andrew cards. The Operation Andrew program is the single most effective method of reaching the unconverted and integrating them into the local church. One survey of Crusade inquirers revealed that 50 percent of those who went forward to receive Christ in response to the evangelist's invitation had been brought to the meetings on *church buses.* The pastor of a large Baptist church in the southwestern United States reported that he had used the delegations and the bus plan, and as a result "in the two-year period following the Crusade our church baptized and received into membership over 200 precious people who had accepted Christ at the Crusade."

6. *Ushers:* Usher leaders are informed of the important role that ushers play in the Crusade. Since an usher is the first person to greet those who attend, his attitude will often influence the attitudes of Crusade attenders. Following a Crusade in his city, the pastor of a Community church noted that "the usher becomes a key person in the Crusade because he is the first one the people are going to see coming inside the stadium. He has to be prayerfully prepared, up-to-date, smiling, and passively aggressive with a cheery note. . . ."

An usher's ability to guide the crowd in a firm cordial manner is also important for their safety. Ushers are challenged to recruit numbers beyond the usual ushering staff of the church to allow others to become involved. Properly presented, the responsibility of ushering can be a challenge to both personal and spiritual excellence.

7. *Women:* Women's leaders are informed that their two primary responsibilities are to develop neighborhood prayer meetings throughout the entire Crusade area, and to involve women in small group Bible studies (nurture groups) for follow-up after the Crusade. The goal is to have neighborhood prayer meetings throughout the city. Women are challenged to recruit others from their churches who will open their homes for prayer. Devotional content and specific prayer requests are communicated to these home prayer meetings through specially prepared radio broadcasts or tape recordings. Although no one can organize prayer, we can organize opportunities for prayer. The women's committee is effective in doing this, often recruiting enough women to open 3,000 to 5,000 homes for prayer in a metropolitan area.

The impact of this great effort to mobilize prayer touches individual lives, as well as the Crusade itself. In Indiana two sisters who hadn't spoken to each other in years were surprised to end up in the same living room for a home prayer meeting. Following the prayer time, one sister walked over to the other, embraced her and asked forgiveness. A spirit of revival prevailed in that prayer group. Following a prayer time in a Kansas household, one lady said, "I need to meet the One I'm praying to. I sense I do not know God as you ladies do." That day Jesus Christ became a personal reality in her life. In Virginia an antagonistic neighbor slammed her door in the face of a woman as she issued a cordial invitation to come to her home for prayer. The neighbor did not come to either the prayer meetings or the Crusade, but several weeks after the meetings had concluded, she rang the doorbell of the prayer hostess' house to tell of her need. She had just found out that her husband had cancer and he had only weeks to live. At 2:00 that morning, through the love and prayer of that hostess, the neighbor found peace with God through Jesus Christ.

8. *Youth:* Youth leaders are challenged to involve the youth members of their church in every phase of the Crusade and to invite them to pre-Crusade youth activities. Since over 60 percent of those going forward at the invitation to accept Christ are under the age of 25, the Youth Committee presents one of the greatest potentials for evangelistic outreach. Generally in Crusade cities youth organize a mini-Crusade committee with emphasis on Operation Andrew, counseling, prayer, visitation.

The results of this involvement are felt in the local church. One minister wrote, "We saw our senior high Monday night class jump in attendance from the low 20s to the 40s. The vitality of the group has increased. In addition, a new college-age Bible class has been formed." Another pastor rejoiced, "Our young people's groups have not only grown numerically, but have become more enthusiastic in their response to the Word of God."

9. *Love-in-Action:* Depending upon the needs and desires of local Crusade leadership, a Love-in-Action Committee is sometimes formed. Church leaders for this committee have the responsibility of involving church members in meaningful service that will apply the love of Christ within the church and the community. Their objective is to channel the spiritual momentum developed through the Crusade effort into practical service after the meetings are over. In some cities a catalog of agencies in need of volunteers is compiled and circulated to the churches, and special seminars are held to orient church members to these opportunities. Often food is collected to be distributed through local church agencies.

Each church leaders' meeting is concluded with a time of prayer. Leaders are urged to start their work immediately. When each one leaves the rally, he has specific goals and deadlines. The value of involvement has been strongly emphasized, and he has received instructions about how to recruit others. Special emphasis has been placed on the fact that this is a local Crusade, and that what each leader does will directly influence the results of the Crusade, both in his local church and in his city. In the days ahead continual follow-up and encouragement is given to each of these leaders to ensure maximum participation by the congregations in the nine areas of Crusade involvement.

In Review:

The following principles of Crusade evangelism are applied through the Leaders' Rally:

1. The evangelist cannot bring a Crusade with him to a city. It is a local effort, and the involvement of

local church leadership is essential.

2. Each church congregation needs to view a Crusade as though its members are personally responsible for its success, and organize the congregation to achieve maximum involvement.

3. Each task is broken down into manageable roles so that the pastor can delegate that role to responsible church members.

4. A pyramid structure of leadership is developed for ever-increasing involvement. Involvement is a key to effective Crusades.

5. Each church leader is asked to set goals and is given specific deadlines for achieving them. There is a regular review of progress in meeting these goals.

7
Promotion:
Factors That Influence Crusade Attendance

One evening during Billy Graham's 1954 London Crusade, the beloved Gospel singer, George Beverly Shea, chose to sing John Peterson's Gospel song:

"It took a miracle to put the stars in place,
It took a miracle to hang the world in space."

Listening to the song, an irate English woman stormed out of the meeting and penned an angry letter to Billy Graham in which she complained, "You have the audacity to come to England at all and tell us how to live, let alone the impertinence to put your soloist up there to sing, 'It took "America" to put the stars in place.' " Since soloist Bev Shea is known for his clear articulation of words, this well illustrates that good communication involves not just what we *say*, but what others *hear* us say, or perhaps what they want to hear us say!

Good communication is particularly essential in the ministry of evangelism. This is true both in presenting the message of the Gospel, and in announcing the occasion where that message can be heard. The Gospel according to Mark records an illustration of this from Jesus' life when He healed a man of leprosy. The man "went out, and began to publish it much, and to blaze abroad the matter, insomuch that Jesus could no more openly enter into the city, but was without in desert places: and they came to him from every quarter. And again he entered into Capernaum after some days; and it was noised that he was in the house. And straightway many were gathered together, insomuch that there was no room to receive them, no, not so much as about the door: and he preached the word unto them" (Mark 1:45–2:2, KJV). Communication in Jesus' day was largely by word of mouth. This proved to be effective in attracting people into the presence of Christ so that He could "preach the word" to them.

Technology has changed our methods of communication, so that today the print and electronic media are equally as important as word of mouth. Publicity and advertising are an essential part of the contemporary evangelistic event. But this raises some relevant questions: How important is it? How much should we depend on it? Does this eliminate person-to-person communication? How should publicity and advertising be applied in Crusade preparations? Isn't the use of promotional techniques an example of relying on secular methods instead of the Holy Spirit in the work of evangelism? These valid questions will be addressed in the pages that follow.

In answering questions about the use of modern media, a proper understanding of the role of publicity and advertising in promoting Crusade evangelism is necessary. Simply put, *publicity* is any exposure that is provided *free* merely by supplying pertinent information. This includes, among other means, posters in churches and public buildings, public service announcements, and bulletin inserts. *Advertising* is any commercial exposure that is *purchased*, such as radio and television time, newspaper advertisements, billboards, and bus signs.

Publicity and advertising are absolutely essential in the development of a Crusade. A proper understanding of what these tools can and cannot do for a Crusade is needed in order to utilize them effectively. Attendance at Crusade services cannot be promoted in the same way as promoting impulse items, such as potato chips or cookies, which sell themselves if properly and conveniently displayed. The prior assumption is that people already have an appetite for the product and it only needs to be attractively packaged and readily available. Rather, motivation to attend a Crusade service is generated at a much deeper level, and often requires both a primary and a secondary influence on the individual. For example, if you feel the need to diet, a widely advertised diet program may attract your attention but not motivate you to action. However, after a friend tells (and shows) you his successful experience with the program, you are more likely to try it yourself.

Goals of Promotion

What should be the goals of Crusade promotion through advertising and publicity? The goals should be in harmony with, and supportive of, Crusade objectives—which are to do evangelism and to strengthen the local church. Advertising and publicity serve these objectives best when they encourage involvement in Crusade preparations, and promote attendance at the Crusade meetings—especially attendance by those whose hearts have been prepared to respond to the Gospel.

There are three key principles to keep in mind when promoting Crusade involvement and attendance. A brief review of these principles (discussed in more detail in Chapter Two) provides the necessary background for our subject.

First, evangelism is the work of the Holy Spirit. Publicity and advertising cannot do that work, but they can be "tools" which the Holy Spirit uses to accomplish His purpose. A major misconception faced in Crusades is that you can build evangelism around a public personality with adequate advertising. Recently, in a North American city, Crusade personnel had a difficult time convincing some local leaders that two full-page ads in the newspaper would not in themselves accomplish the objectives of a Crusade. Such a superficial approach would have yielded limited attendance, and few spiritual inquirers.

Second, evangelism is built on relationships. It is possible to gather a crowd at a Crusade by making the meetings entertaining and appealing. But for an evangelistic harvest to occur, Christians must sow and water in the lives of people around them. *The living example and the loving invitation of a Christian, offered to someone who needs Jesus Christ, is the single most important factor in influencing attendance.*

Third, involvement produces commitment. People who become involved in the Crusade preparations will be committed to its goals, to prayer, and to inviting others. Around this circle of committed people is a larger circle of the lives they touch. The larger the inner core of involved persons, the larger will be the number who are influenced and invited by them. For this reason, *involvement is the primary strategy for promoting Crusade attendance.*

Research in Crusade Promotion

In addition to thirty-five years of practical experience in Crusade evangelism, BGEA has commissioned careful research; the conclusions of the research supported these principles. Dr. Larry Caillouet of Western Kentucky University, who wrote his doctoral dissertation on "Comparative Media Effectiveness in an Evangelistic Campaign," has conducted three Crusade surveys involving Billy Graham Association personnel.

Dr. Caillouet's surveys had two primary objectives: (1) to learn how people become *aware* of a Crusade; and (2) to determine what motivates them to *attend*. He subdivided awareness and motivation into two categories: mass media and interpersonal media. Mass media include newspapers, radio, television, billboards, bus signs. Interpersonal media include church announcements, conversations at church, information from family members, information from friends.

As a result of his surveys, he concluded that *awareness* of a Crusade in a community is influenced largely through the mass media and, in particular, through newspapers which not only carry advertising, but extensive news coverage. However, *attendance* at the Crusade is influenced primarily by interpersonal factors. In summary comments about the Crusade in Edmonton, Alberta, Dr. Caillouet said, "Taken as a whole, these figures are strong proof that while the mass media are very effective in delivering information and producing awareness of an evangelistic Crusade, they are fairly ineffective in influencing attendance at the Crusade even when the evangelist is extremely well known. In the absence of interpersonal contacts, very few people are motivated to attend the Crusade." (See Appendix F for more complete statistical information.)

These conclusions apply to a North American, English-speaking culture and should not be generally applied to other cultures or media mixtures. For example, in other developed nations, the type and availability of various media for religious purposes is often limited. This would influence the effectiveness of media exposure. In undeveloped nations which are not satiated with entertainment opportunities or media stimuli, often even simple posters and word-of-mouth are effective in gathering large crowds. Curiosity becomes a much more significant factor in such settings. Billy Graham Crusades in undeveloped countries have consistently shown that proportionately much larger attendance will result from a much smaller expenditure for media than in developed nations.

Mass Media Benefits

Dr. Caillouet points out that although the mass media is not the primary influence on Crusade attendance, they play a significant role. In fact, he suggests that the mass media serve five important functions in Crusades:

1. Mass media confer a sense of legitimacy on the Crusade. The average person concludes that when there is extensive coverage of an event in the city, it must be a significant event.
2. Mass media reinforce the supporters of the Crusade. They are encouraged to invite others because of that reinforcement.
3. Mass media serve as a conversation starter. Talking about the Crusade opens the door to personal witnessing.
4. Mass media can plant the idea of attending in the minds of people who might not otherwise attend the Crusade.
5. Mass media continue to raise the spiritual consciousness of a community, beyond the immediate context of the Crusade—at least for some members of the community—and enhance post-Crusade witnessing opportunities.

Briefly stated, mass media help plant the idea, interpersonal contact prompts the person to act on that idea. The two are an effective combination.

The results of Dr. Caillouet's survey reveal in conclusive terms that although mass media are important and there is a definite need to create community awareness for an evangelistic event, it should be considered as just one oar of the boat. If you row with only one oar, you will make little progress and are likely to go around in circles. The other oar is the emphasis placed on Christians inviting their friends and neighbors who need the message of Christ. There is a limit to the help you can expect from advertising alone. Once there is adequate exposure in the community, the expenditure of additional advertising dollars will only be wasted. But even money spent for adequate exposure may be wasted if Christians are not pulling on that "other oar" of personal invitation. The appropriate choice about mass media and interpersonal contact is not either/or, but one plus the other.

This research has provided a basis for strengthening both aspects of Crusade promotion—mass media and interpersonal contacts. Crusade leaders seek to dispel misconceptions about what advertising can do, and emphasize the importance of the personal invitation. Since Operation Andrew is the most effective means of encouraging personal invitations, new materials and bulletin inserts have been created to keep this emphasis continually before church members. Newspaper ads and radio spots are produced to challenge Christians to invite their friends to the meetings. In addition, advertising materials are designed to speak to some of man's universal needs, such as loneliness, emptiness, hopelessness, as well as marriage and family problems. These ads are intended to touch the reader at his point of need. They also remind Christians that needy people are all around and motivate Christians to invite them to the Crusade services.

Although the research is conclusive and the strategy has proved effective, there are exceptions to every rule. During the 1982 Crusade in Boston, a young woman with time to waste was standing on Commonwealth Avenue across from the Crusade site. A piece of paper blew across the street and stuck to the toe of her shoe. When she pulled off the paper, she saw that it was a brochure about the Crusade meetings and she decided to attend. That night, after listening to the Gospel message, she went forward to receive Christ as her personal Savior. God is sovereign. He not only blesses those strategies of evangelism which rely on Him, He goes beyond their limitations to fulfill His purposes in the lives of others.

The Use of Publicity

Strategic use of publicity is equally as important as advertising. The application of publicity needs to be viewed with two target audiences in mind: the internal audience (the supporting Christian community), and the external audience (the community at large). If there are six months of preparation for a Crusade, 90 percent of the emphasis in publicity is placed on internal communication for the first five-and-one-half months. The purpose is to build involvement and commitment on the part of Christians, which will motivate them to attend and to invite others. Also, internal publicity interests uninvolved church members to attend—many of whom may need to make a commitment to Christ.

Although public exposure through the media, which informs the community at large, is welcomed and sought during the early stages of preparation, it is not necessary to advertise intensely until the meetings are close at hand. (See Figure 4 in Appendix F.) Bulletin inserts, pastoral announcements, posters, mailings, and fliers are used to communicate to the internal (church) community. This communication is coordinated to allow for one primary emphasis each month and is scheduled to avoid interfering with major church events. (See Figure 3 in Appendix F.)

Anticipating Crusade Attendance

It is not possible to predict accurately Crusade attendance, but we do have some advance indicators. The best attendance predictor is the group delegation requests for reserved section tickets. Although tickets are not needed to attend the Crusade meetings, which are always free, they are a good tool for Christians to use when inviting non-Christian friends to attend with them. A church delegation with tickets will be able to get seats in the same section. The total of these delegation requests indicate the number of churches and groups planning to come and bring uncommitted friends with them.

Generally, the attendance pattern parallels (usually higher, sometimes lower) these ticket requests, except when there is a well-known guest featured or the weather is extremely bad. Attendance on the closing or opening Sunday and holiday weekends will also vary from this guideline. Generally speaking, if preparations are adequate, group delegations provide a reliable estimate of anticipated Crusade attendance.

How Much Advertising Is Needed?

The amount of advertising needed is usually determined by keeping five factors in view: (1) the size of the meeting facility; (2) the strength in numbers and commitment of the involved churches; (3) the size of the group delegation requests; (4) traffic congestion and available parking; and (5) the amount of free media exposure experienced or anticipated.

If the meetings are held in a small auditorium with good parking, a large base of Christians involved in preparations, strong group delegation requests, and good support from the media, then advertising can be kept at a minimum. Advertising extensively when it is not possible to seat all the people who come is poor stewardship and a poor witness. On the other hand, if the Crusade is in a large stadium with limited parking, a smaller base of Christian support and involvement, weak media support, and group delegations that predict far less than stadium capacity, then additional advertising is not only warranted but necessary.

Is Promotion Unspiritual?

The use of the promotional tools of advertising and publicity is sometimes criticized as being "unspiritual." Advertising and publicity in themselves are amoral. It is how and why they are used that determine whether they serve "spiritual" or "unspiritual" purposes. Advertising and publicity are not to be seen as some secular device to be employed along with the "spiritual weapons" of a Crusade. Nor should the use of media be viewed as an accommodation of secular techniques, thus implying that one can fulfill spiritual objectives with human resources. Rather, advertising and publicity should be seen as tools available under the control of the Holy Spirit to communicate both the event where the message will be preached as well as the message of the Gospel itself. In light of this, the application of media resources should be done with awareness of their strengths and weaknesses, and most of all with earnest prayer that God will empower these tools to an effectiveness that far exceeds any human expectations (Ephesians 3:20).

In Review:

Three primary factors influence Crusade attendance:
1. *Publicity and Advertising*—Research has shown that a limited percentage of the general public will attend Crusade services because of publicity and advertising alone. However, good publicity and ad-

vertising are essential to create an image, build credibility, prepare people to receive an invitation, and to encourage Christians to fulfill their responsibility of inviting others.

2. *Involvement*—The larger the circle of people involved in some responsibility, the greater will be the surrounding circle of their relationships. This direct involvement will have a significant influence on sustained attendance at the Crusade meetings. For this reason, 90 percent of the pre-Crusade publicity is directed internally to the church.

3. *Personal Invitation*—Research has shown that at least two out of every three persons who attend Crusade meetings and nearly three of every four who come forward have been personally invited. For effective evangelism there is no substitute for the committed Christian inviting and bringing his friends to the meetings.

8

Preservation:

Turning Decisions Into Disciples

President and Mrs. Lyndon B. Johnson were among the crowd of 61,000 in the closing service in the Houston Astrodome. "The First Lady, seeing so many come forward in that last service of the Houston Crusade, and recalling that 10,000 others had already joined that penitent band during the week, said, 'Wonderful, wonderful! But what happens now?' "[1]

In New Testament evangelism, proclaiming the Gospel and inviting people to make a "decision for Christ" is only the beginning. Like graduation from college, it is a "commencement." As one leader has declared, it's the "starting gun," not the "finishing flag." The Great Commission mandates that we "make disciples." This is implicit in the definition of evangelism prepared by the Anglican Archbishops Committee in 1918: "To evangelize is so to present Christ Jesus in the power of the Holy Spirit that men shall come to put their trust in God through Him, to accept Him as their Savior, *and serve Him as their King in the fellowship of His Church*" (italics mine). Two working groups of the Lausanne Committee have accepted a definition of evangelism which includes: "The *goal* of evangelism is to persuade men and women to become disciples of Jesus Christ and to serve Him in the fellowship of His Church."[2]

These definitions strongly affirm that a key objective of effective evangelism is "disciples" who demonstrate their commitment to Christ by their commitment to a local body of believers.

The Crusade follow-up process for fulfilling that goal is best understood by a review of: (1) the biblical basis of follow-up; (2) social change and follow-up; and (3) the programs and priorities for follow-up.

The Biblical Basis of Follow-Up

Follow-up may be defined as giving continued attention to a new Christian (new baby in Christ) while he is being integrated into the church, discovering his place of service, developing his full potential for Jesus Christ, and beginning to help build Christ's Church. Although this may sound idealistic, it is a pattern set forth in Ephesians for reaching the lost and building the church. The apostle Paul wrote, "Some of us have been given special ability as apostles; to others [God] has given the gift of being able to preach well; some have special ability in winning people to Christ, helping them to trust him as their Savior; still others have a gift for caring for God's people as a shepherd does his sheep, leading and teaching them in the ways of God. Why is it that he gives us these special abilities to do certain things best? It is that God's people will be equipped to do better work for him, building up the church, the body of Christ, to a position of strength and maturity; until finally we all believe alike about our salvation and about our Savior, God's Son, and all become full-grown in the Lord—yes, to the point of being filled full with Christ" (Ephesians 4:11–13, TLB).

That greatest missionary evangelist, the apostle Paul, models for us both the spirit and the principles of New Testament follow-up. His chief concern was for the growth and development of new Christians. His goal was for their maturity. "O my dear children, I am suffering a mother's birth pangs for you again, until Christ is formed in you" (Galatians 4:19, Williams). To the Colossians, he announced, "We proclaim Him, admonishing every man . . . with all wisdom, that we may present every man complete in Christ" (Colossians 1:28, NASB). Paul, through his letters, kept in constant touch with churches and individuals, pouring out his love to them. "For to this end also did I write, that I might know the proof of you, whether ye be obedient in all things" (2 Corinthians 2:9, KJV).

Paul's prayers reveal his longing to be with people, ministering to them and their needs. He prayed long and often for their spiritual growth. "Night and day praying exceedingly that we might see your face, and might perfect that which is lacking in your faith" (1 Thessalonians 3:10, KJV). When he could not go personally, he sent men whom he had trained. "So when I could not bear it any longer, I decided to be left behind in Athens alone, and so I sent my brother Timothy, God's minister in the preaching of the good news of Christ, to strengthen and encourage you in your faith, so that none of you might be deceived amid these difficulties" (1 Thessalonians 3:1–3, Williams).

Of utmost importance was Paul's love and concern for new Christians. He was willing to become involved in their lives regardless of the cost. "Because we were yearning for you so tenderly, we were willing, not only to share with you God's good news, but to lay down our very lives too for you, all because you were so dearly loved by us" (1 Thessalonians 2:8, Williams). *The unwillingness by too many of us to give of ourselves and our time to become vitally involved with a new Christian may be one of the greatest obstacles to follow-up today.*

The precedent is clearly set. New Christians do need care, and that care should be administered by someone. The one who cares enough to bring that person to hear the Gospel, and/or the one who leads him to Christ is the most logical person to work with the new Christian. That person should provide further spiritual help and counsel as well as encourage good devotional habits and regular church attendance. He becomes a "spiritual parent" for this new baby in Christ. *That means being available!*

Social Change and Follow-Up

The biblical strategy for fulfilling the Great Commission mandate has always been for the church to "go" to those who have not heard the good news. The early church went out and proclaimed the Gospel wherever they could get a hearing—in homes, synagogues, marketplaces, public forums, prisons, everywhere! Those who responded were gathered into little caring circles of growing believers who made up the church of that day—a church without buildings, but a living organism. The mandate did not change in the early days of modern evangelism—the days of Whitefield, Wesley, Finney, and Moody. Neither has the strategy changed. These evangelists went wherever they could get a hearing—to churches, public buildings, brush arbors, the fields, the marketplace, the street corners.

Since Adam's rebellion in the Garden of Eden, people's need of a Savior has remained unchanged. But society has changed dramatically.

In the early eighteenth and nineteenth centuries the United States was more rural and agrarian than urban. The church had a strong identity within society, both in physical buildings and through moral influence. Social customs often reflected the value system of the church. Those who responded to the

Gospel understood that they should attend church. This was presumed of those who "had religion" and even by those who rejected Christianity. This meant that new converts usually attended church.

Today society is basically urban, not rural. Yet the mandate for evangelism is the same, and man's need is the same, even if society is changing. It is generally acknowledged that we no longer have a Sunday school generation. The church does not have the same distinctive place in the minds of many urbanized North Americans. Neither does it have the same moral influence on our values. Society has become more complex with advancing technology, shifting dramatically from a largely agrarian and rural society to an urban and cosmopolitan population. With that has come increasing secularism, if not humanism.

A result of the changing societal picture is that a commitment to Christ is not automatically associated with attendance at church. People who have been reached through personal evangelism do not necessarily have roots in the church, nor do they feel the cultural momentum to identify with a local body of believers. This means that greater effort must be put forth in the 1980s than in the 1780s, the 1880s, or even the 1950s to ensure that those who make commitments to Christ are integrated into a church.

Just as the methods (but not the essential message) of proclamation have changed to adapt to a changing society and new technology, so the methods of preservation also need to be adapted as society changes. Over the past thirty-five years Billy Graham Crusades have gone through a progression of methods in order to conserve more effectively the results and to integrate inquirers into the local church so that the ultimate goal, "making disciples," can be effectively achieved.

The principles involved in Crusade evangelism are important in fulfilling the commitments to make disciples. First, Crusade evangelism is built on personal relationships—which means a link is already established for personal follow-up and discipleship. Second, Crusade evangelism serves the church as it is represented by many individual local bodies. People who attend the Crusade meetings are often brought by church members, thus providing an immediate link to the local body when they respond to the Gospel of Jesus Christ. Third, the message includes the cost of following Christ as Lord and Savior and emphasizes the need for commitment. Fourth, training, methods, and materials on discipleship are provided to the local churches so that they can more effectively disciple the inquirers after the meetings are over. Although Crusade evangelism cannot and should not be the sole discipling agency, it can and should be linked to local churches so that discipleship will be part of the natural flow of events following a Crusade.

In earlier centuries evangelists put less emphasis on methods or materials for discipleship. This was no doubt because society was not as complex, the church had a stronger identity in society, and there was almost a cultural pressure in assuring that those who made "decisions" would go to church. But the structures of society have changed dramatically, requiring substantial changes in the approach to follow-up.

Billy Graham has seen the need for follow-up in a modern society and has taken firm steps to meet that need. As Waldron Scott has written, "It is to Billy Graham's lasting credit that he, more than any other public evangelist in the late '40s and early '50s, perceived this connection. Early in his ministry Graham wrote, 'I have come to the conclusion that the most important phase [of an evangelistic campaign] is the follow-up.' "[3] For help Graham turned to Dawson Trotman, founder and then president of The Navigators, a movement specializing in discipling. John Pollock, Graham's biographer, noted the collaboration of Trotman and Graham in 1951. He wrote that it "may have been one of those little-known, unrecognized but decisive moments in the growth of the Christian church."[4]

Scott continued, "The fundamental objective of Graham's follow-up program was not merely to get a person to come forward and register a decision for Christ, but to help solidify that decision and insure that the individual became an integral part of a local congregation. There his Christian life would be nourished, and his spiritual gifts developed and employed. If, as is generally conceded, an exceptionally high percentage of men, women, and children coming to Christ in a Graham Crusade go on to experience a life of spiritual fulfillment, recognition must be paid to Graham's early discernment that the true object of evangelism, in the context of the Great Commission, is discipleship."[5]

Just as society, technology, and the church have continued to change since 1951 when Graham and Trotman first met, so have the methods and materials of follow-up in Billy Graham's Crusades. Crusade leaders have sought to adapt to the changing needs in order to continue effective discipling. In light of the sociological trends of the last 100 years Crusade evangelism will undoubtedly need to exert even more effort in the future to keep the same proportion of inquirers growing in Jesus Christ.

Unfortunately, some church growth proponents have chosen to interpret Crusade data negatively and have made church growth methodology competitive with Crusade evangelism instead of complementary. In my opinion, conservation is not an issue of one method versus the other. All methods are needed. The circumstances determine the choices. To win baseball games the manager's choice of which players to use is not between a pitcher or a catcher, but rather in how to use the best abilities of both. It seems that the need of the church today is not so much that of choosing one method over another, but more of getting all the good we can from each method, while understanding its strengths and limitations in fulfilling the goal of making disciples.

Programs and Priorities for Follow-Up

In order for effective follow-up to take place, we cannot simply assume that the average Christian involved in a Crusade has the understanding, the training, or the materials for good follow-up. Thus, training in proven methods and providing carefully developed materials are essential. This process of preparing for preservation begins early in the pre-Crusade scheduling. The development of nurture group leaders, Christian Life and Witness class training and special follow-up seminars, as well as the communication of materials and methods and the planning for post-Crusade activities, are all part of the process of Crusade development which is aimed at responsible discipleship once the Crusade is over.

This raises the question of who is responsible for the discipleship of Crusade inquirers: the evangelist, the local Crusade committee, or the local church. That question was asked by Vanderbilt sociologist Dr. Glenn Firebaugh in a survey of pastors following the 1976 Seattle Billy Graham Crusade. Nine out of ten (91 percent) thought the local church had primary responsibility, 7 percent believed that the local Crusade committee was responsible, and only 2 percent thought that the Billy Graham Association should be responsible. Actually, it should be a partnership in which each agency is fully committed to the goals of effective follow-up.

Multiple Approach to Follow-Up

Billy Graham Crusades have adopted a multiple approach to follow-up, offering many different methods in the hope that one or more will be effective in the life of the inquirer. Primary emphasis is given to personal follow-up, especially through the local church, but there are at least eight follow-up activities offered in every Crusade setting (see Figure 1).

First, Personal Counseling. A clear commitment to Jesus Christ as Savior is the first step in follow-up. Unfortunately, in some evangelistic efforts, the invitation to accept Christ is not made clear, and people respond to an appeal without their real needs being met. This becomes evident in the follow-up, and may result in the inquirer becoming a "spiritual drop-out."

Effective follow-up can take place only in the life

Crusade Follow-Up Programs

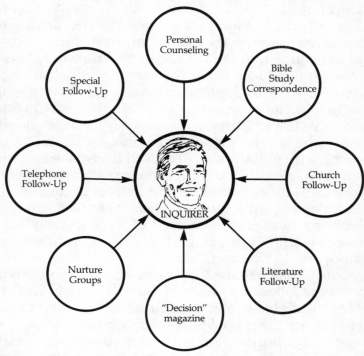

Figure 1.

of a person who has been truly born again by the Spirit of God. When the Holy Spirit is at work in the life of an individual, convicting and regenerating, then we can say with assurance, "Being confident of this very thing, that he which hath begun a good work in you will perform it until the day of Jesus Christ" (Philippians 1:6, KJV).

Personal counseling is an immeasurable help in any meeting where people are invited to receive Christ. Mature counselors with a command of Scripture who are able to understand a person's need can be used of the Holy Spirit to make an inquirer's decision clear. These counselors can introduce a person to the Bible study material and later follow up those whom they have counseled.

In Crusades people are trained to give personal counsel at the time of the inquirer's decision and to follow up those inquirers afterward. The degree of help given, of course, will depend on the maturity and the concern of the counselor and the willingness of the inquirer to receive that help. Some years ago when we were in South America, a missionary who was helping as a counselor told us that he had committed his life to Christ five years earlier in Scotland. He said his counselor was still praying for him and helping with his support. This is an unusual situation, but we have found through the years that counselors in our Crusades are faithful and helpful in counseling and following up inquirers. Counselors are asked to telephone, write, or visit each of the inquirers they counsel within 48 hours, and send the Crusade office a report of that contact.

Second, Bible Study Correspondence. An important part of the follow-up program is the "Living in Christ" Bible study given to each inquirer at the time of his commitment. This booklet, which contains the Gospel of John, Scripture memory verses, devotional reading, and a series of question-and-answer Bible studies, helps the inquirer clarify his commitment. The material is aimed at answering the questions an inquirer might have following his commitment and is designed to give him a simple but firm anchor for his faith. Many churches throughout the world are now using this material for follow-up. Numerous situations have been reported where this Bible study not only settled and strengthened the inquirer's decision, but also was used to bring others in his immediate family to faith in Christ.

Third, Church Follow-Up. The most important aspect of follow-up is the personal care of a local church. The local church has the responsibility of discipling and nurturing those who have made Christian commitments, encouraging them with warm and loving support. Each evening following the Crusade service, information from the counseling card is placed on a Minister's Information Form and mailed to the church listed as a preference by the inquirer. It is Crusade policy that these be in the mail that same night. The pastor or his designated representative is asked to contact each inquirer within seventy-two hours of receipt of the information, and report the results of that call to the follow-up committee. The caller is asked to clarify the inquirer's commitment, encourage him in his Christian walk, and seek to bring him into the life of the local fellowship.

Fourth, Literature Follow-Up. A few days after his commitment an inquirer receives a letter of encouragement from Dr. Graham with further study helps. This is designed to reinforce the commitment while more personal contacts are being made.

Fifth, "Decision" Magazine. For one year following the Crusade each inquirer receives "Decision" magazine as a gift from the Billy Graham Association. This magazine has messages by Dr. Graham, articles on the Christian life, articles by Bible teachers, testimonies, and other materials to strengthen the inquirer's faith.

Sixth, Nurture Groups. A small-group prayer and Bible study fellowship through the local church provides a good opportunity for the new Christian to grow in his faith. These Bible study fellowships are called nurture groups. Meeting on a regular basis with other new Christians to share what God is doing in their lives is an enriching experience for the new believers.

Each member covenants to pray daily for others in the study group, works in a Bible study lesson book, and shares with other group members in a discussion-type study. The lessons in these studies deal with assurance of salvation, the Lordship of Christ, the authority of the Bible, effective prayer, walking in the Spirit, witnessing, and many other topics. Weekly assigned projects help each individual establish a daily quiet time and become involved in ministering to others.

The leaders of the nurture group are trained prior to the Crusade. Once a week for several weeks hundreds of Christians meet in groups of ten to become familiar with the lesson material and the techniques in leading a discussion. Having had this experience, they have greater confidence in leading follow-up nurture groups after the Crusade is over.

The Billy Graham Evangelistic Association has developed several discipleship tools to be used by churches in follow-up: "Roots," "30 Discipleship Exercises," "Living in Christ." Also, a Bible study series for teenagers covers the same general areas as the discipleship studies. However, a different approach allows a teenager more versatility in doing his lessons. This makes the discussion-type study more attractive and interesting to teens, yet it is biblical and basic to the Christian life.

Seventh, Telephone Follow-Up. To make absolutely certain that every inquirer has been contacted and given further help, a post-Crusade survey has been developed. About three weeks after the Crusade ends, every inquirer possible (excluding children ages one through eleven) is called on the telephone by a trained worker. Questions are asked about his growth in Christ and, if the inquirer is progressing well, the interview takes no more than a few minutes. This interview provides opportunity to give further counseling when required.

Through this telephone survey we are able to enlist many more people in the Bible study nurture program and give additional help to the inquirer. They are encouraged to become established in a local church. This may appear to be a duplication of effort, since both the pastor and the counselor have been asked to contact the inquirer, but our experience indicates that not only is the survey necessary, the inquirer appreciates the call.

Eighth, Special Follow-Up. The need for special follow-up programs varies from Crusade to Crusade. Some examples of special follow-up programs are Bible studies conducted for students in their homes or school dormitories; military at their installations and professional men and women in their places of business. Women involved in the Crusade prayer program are encouraged to continue meeting once a week for prayer and Bible study and to invite Crusade inquirers to attend. Sometimes personal enrichment seminars are scheduled, and inquirers are invited to a day of training and fellowship. Special follow-up is always tailored to meet the particular needs of the Crusade area and its constituency.

Offering proven methods and materials alone will not ensure effective follow-up. They must be diligently and prayerfully applied. One pastor wrote, "The follow-up program of Billy Graham Crusades is an excellent one. We followed the 'book' and had good results. We gained a high percentage of the referrals made to us. But then, we also worked at it. In the Lutheran church our people are accustomed to making calls, and they are not afraid to follow through."

Referral Priorities and Policy

Two priorities govern follow-up activities in Crusade evangelism. These priorities are (1) the spiritual growth of the inquirer; and (2) maintaining healthy relationships between churches. The referral policy for relating inquirers to local churches has been shaped in light of these priorities.

Those who respond to the evangelist's invitation are called "inquirers" for although we know they are seeking spiritual help, only the Holy Spirit knows precisely the type of commitment they are making. In requesting information for the counseling card, counselors ask inquirers for their church preference or the name of the church they attend regularly. If they do not have a church preference or a church home, they are asked, "Which church brought you to the Crusade?" The information is recorded on the counseling card exactly as given and goes to the follow-up department. Information from these cards is then sent to local churches according to guidelines shaped by the follow-up priorities.

1. When an inquirer names a participating church (as determined by the local follow-up committee) as his stated preference, information is sent to that church for follow-up of the inquirer.
2. When inquirers do not have a church preference or a church home, information is sent to a participating church closest to the inquirer's home address.
3. When inquirers name a sect, cult, or non-Christian relationship as their religious preference, information is sent to a participating church closest to the inquirer's home address.

Sending Inquirers to "Cold" Churches

The most common criticism of follow-up procedures is that inquirers are sometimes sent back to spiritually "cold" churches. In responding to that statement, we need to review:

1. The follow-up committee does not and cannot "refer" or assign inquirers to churches in the sense that a patient is referred (sent) from one doctor to another. Rather, "information" about the inquirer is communicated to a local pastor who is asked to help the inquirer become established in his or her Christian faith and become active in the local congregation.

2. It is unethical to assign people to another church if they already have a Christian church home. An attempt to reassign inquirers may hinder or cut off completely the opportunity for that individual to receive other follow-up help which is provided on a personal or neighborhood basis.

3. Mailing information from a counseling card to a church does not guarantee that the person named on that "information form" will go to that church. Inquirers often have life relationships and loyalties in religious and cultural settings which cannot be changed quickly. Just as it is unrealistic to ask a baby to choose where he can find the best food, clothing, and shelter, so it is often unrealistic to expect a spiritual baby to know whether he needs to change his church in order be properly nurtured in the faith. That is why a number of other follow-up steps, including neighborhood Bible studies, are used to nurture an inquirer even if he maintains his current church home.

Behind the question of referral to "cold" churches is a prior question: "Should we attempt to reach people with the Gospel if we cannot guarantee that they will have a good church home after they make a commitment to Jesus Christ?" An answer to that question requires placing in proper perspective the problem of controlling an inquirer's spiritual environment after he has responded to Christ.

Generally speaking, what takes place in the local church is also what happens on a city-wide basis in cooperative evangelism. Only the magnitude of the event is changed. A review of the implied philosophy of handling "spiritual commitments" in the local church will aid us in understanding how it must be handled across the whole metropolitan area.

Take, for example, the church in upstate New York which for years has had a radio broadcast across the western part of the state. Many people have heard the Gospel through that broadcast, yet they live too far from that church ever to think of attending regularly. Others who listen to it might never choose that church simply for reasons of personal preference. Should the church be spreading the Gospel over such a wide area if they cannot guarantee the spiritual environment of those who may commit themselves to Christ through that ministry?

Members of that church are encouraged to witness to Christ where they live, work, and shop. In their witnessing and soul winning, they have no guarantee that if they lead someone to Christ that person will end up in their church or some other evangelical church. Should they be discouraged from witnessing because they cannot control the church environment of those who might respond?

That church annually conducts a daily vacation Bible school in which a large percentage of those attending are children who do not regularly attend that church. Every year some of these children "invite Jesus into their hearts," but the majority of them do not end up attending the church. Should the church restrict its programs only to those who regularly attend in order to guarantee control of their spiritual environment? Those questions have never arisen in that congregation. The issue has been, "How can we share the good news of Christ with more people?" The church makes every reasonable effort to disciple those who respond and incorporate them into the life of the congregation. But they have never let their inability to do that perfectly with everyone limit their highest priority which is spreading the Gospel.

The Holy Spirit and Follow-Up

Jesus said, "Go . . . and preach the gospel" (Mark 16:15, KJV). That is our commission whether or not we ever have the privilege of discipling those who hear and respond. In the book of Acts we read that Philip approached the Ethiopian eunuch, led him to faith in Christ, and baptized him. Then "the Spirit of the Lord suddenly took Philip away, and the eunuch did not see him again" (Acts 8:39, NIV). Philip left immediately with no knowledge of how the new believer would be followed up or where he would have fellowship. The Holy Spirit does not have one single pattern for all follow-up activities. So it is in Crusade evangelism. Every responsible effort should be made to assist those who come forward in their spiritual growth. But, if for reasons beyond our control they are temporarily left in a church which is "cold" spiritually, we can trust the Holy Spirit to use other follow-up activities to help them grow in Christ.

There is ample evidence that the Holy Spirit is trustworthy for this task. Reports by Dr. Robert O. Ferm indicate that "extensive investigations . . . among thousands of inquirers at Billy Graham Crusades have shown that an encouragingly high percentage continue and grow in their commitments."[6] As Dr. Ferm has said, not all seed falls on good soil but "of those who were truly converted, 85 percent are actively involved in the life of the church ten, fifteen and even twenty years later." The significance of these statistics is best understood when contrasted with the results of those who become church members through traditional means. George Sweazey has said, "The saddest figures in all the statistics of American churches are those which tell us that, of every two persons received on profession of faith, one has been dropped as a failure."[7]

Recently a Canadian pastor told me his story. As a teenager he had made a commitment at a Billy Graham Crusade in Toronto, Ontario. When he went back to his "cold" church and began to share his new faith with others in his Sunday school class, the church leaders asked him to stop. Although his parents were not believers, they so valued what they saw in his life that they changed churches, and eventually came to know Christ too. Today he pastors one of the largest churches in his city.

The Great Follow-Up Agent

In the final analysis, the Holy Spirit is the great follow-up agent. Ron Brown was active in his home church, but unconverted. While he was a sophomore at his high school in Lowell, Massachusetts, Billy Graham was holding his 1957 Crusade in New York City. The press coverage of the event was appealing to Ron, and so he urged his family to take a weekend trip to New York City. They arrived three hours early to get into the Yankee Stadium meeting and sat in scorching heat of over 100 degrees. People were jammed in. Even the field, right up to the platform, was full. After the message was preached, Ron recalls, "Through the moving of the Holy Spirit, I made my own personal commitment to Jesus Christ as Lord and Savior. I recall at the time there was no way that a counselor could get to us. We were simply asked by Dr. Graham to stand in our place, which I was moved to do. I was not even able to leave an address or receive any materials."

Back in Lowell, he told his pastor about his decision for Christ. His pastor scoffed at the idea—saying it was just an emotional experience that he would soon get over. Ron goes on to say, "I felt that something had begun in my life that would not let go of me. Of course, now I realize it was the Holy Spirit. It is the Holy Spirit who has developed me as His disciple over these many years. As a result of my warm friendship with my pastor, someone who has an earned doctorate and is well respected as an intellectual, I soon discovered that we were both really praying together for the Lord's guidance. Eventually, he made his own personal commitment. It amazes me how the Holy Spirit led in that way."

Ron went on to a Christian college and then to seminary and was ordained as a minister. When Dr. Graham had his second New York City Crusade (1969–1970), Ron made contact with the Team and became one of Associate Evangelist Leighton Ford's Crusade Directors. While Ron was directing the Des Moines, Iowa, Crusade for Dr. Ford, his parents visited the meetings. There his father went forward and made his own commitment to Christ as Savior. Later, while serving on the staff of Gordon College in New England, Ron had a key role in the development of the six-state outreach for the 1982 New England Crusade. Indeed, the work of the Holy Spirit is the ultimate ingredient in the follow-up process.

In Review:

1. Follow-up is primarily the responsibility of the local church. In order to be properly prepared church pastors and church leaders need both training and materials for discipleship and nurture.
2. A multiple approach is used in Crusade follow-up to offer inquirers a variety of support activities to encourage their Christian growth. The most im-

portant element is personal follow-up by the local church.

3. The Holy Spirit is the great follow-up agent. Even if other means of follow-up cannot be offered, the Gospel should still be preached—trusting the Holy Spirit to care for the "fruit."

9

Product:

Lasting Benefits for the Local Church

Since records of Billy Graham's ministry were first kept in 1947, he has preached face to face to more than one hundred million people in Crusades and other speaking engagements around the world. More than two million have publicly responded to his call to make a commitment to Jesus Christ. In addition, through television, radio, and the printed page, he has communicated the good news of the Gospel to additional hundreds of millions. Uncounted numbers of these, known only to God, have made commitments to Jesus Christ. But the question is still asked, "Do the results last?" Are these merely numbers, or are there "changed lives" behind these statistics? Are there lasting benefits for the local church?

Defining the Results

To answer that question we need to define what we mean by results or benefits from a Crusade. The two stated objectives of a Crusade are to evangelize the community by using a variety of methods and to strengthen the local church for witness and discipleship. Critics of Crusade evangelism have sometimes challenged that mass evangelism does not result in immediate church growth. Most pastors, however, are more patient and apparently more objective. Beyond the addition of numbers, they also see the increased spiritual vitality and strength of a congregation as part of a Crusade's long-term benefits. This was confirmed through research for a doctoral dissertation by Dr. Tom Phillips, who surveyed pastors and congregational leaders following the Memphis Mid-South Crusade in May, 1978. It was further substantiated by the research of Vanderbilt University sociologist, Dr. Glenn Firebaugh, who studied the impact of the Pacific Northwest Billy Graham Crusade in Seattle three-and-one-half years after the event took place.

Dr. Phillips' research pointed to seven benefits that pastors determined were of primary importance to their local ministry: preparatory training, unity of Christians, emphasis on evangelism, spiritual renewal, new additions to the church, new awareness of church and community needs, and the emphasis on prayer. These benefits of Crusade evangelism are evident not only in Memphis, but throughout the world.

Preparatory Training

Ministers cite the training of their laity as the single most significant benefit of a Crusade. People trained in counseling, follow-up, and the prayer ministries continue to use what they have learned in their churches. The church benefits not only during the Crusade, but before it begins and long afterward. This is particularly true of training received through the "Christian Life and Witness" and "Discipleship" programs taught by Crusade personnel. Following the Pacific Northwest Crusade, 55 percent of the ministers surveyed noted that the Christian Life and Witness Classes were effective in training their church members in evangelistic counseling and witnessing. The laypeople themselves who were involved in the Crusade gave an even higher rating, with 82 percent claiming it was beneficial.

In an article on the impact of Billy Graham Crusades, Dr. Lewis Drummond, professor of evangelism at Southern Baptist Theological Seminary, stated, "One of the startling statistics that spring out of the counselor training program is that an average of 20 percent of the trainees who go through the entire program make decisions for Christ themselves. Ten percent of these are first-time decisions. Furthermore, the lives of ministers and thousands of laymen have been revolutionized through several weeks of training in how to lead others to vital faith in Jesus Christ—a definite plus for a local church."[1]

Dr. Donald Gill, executive director of the Evangelistic Association of New England, commented on this impact from a six-state regional Crusade across the New England region in the spring of 1982. Gill stated, "The Crusade results go far beyond the immediate additions to church membership. In the long run it may be much more significant that some 18,000 Christians across New England took part in the counselor training classes. This reservoir of active Christians . . . represents an important asset to the ongoing work of the churches throughout this six-state region. This asset which has great significance often goes unnoticed."

Unity of Christians

One consistent result of Crusade evangelism has been the unifying of Christians—across denominational lines—through their commitment to a common goal: the proclaiming of the Gospel of Jesus Christ. This brings to leadership and laity alike a new sense of expectancy and a new experience in unity. According to Dr. Drummond, "The Crusades appear to give birth to an evangelistic ecumenism as no other effort does. Evangelicals unite wholeheartedly in the quest to win people to Christ."[2]

A layman from the 1976 Seattle Crusade expressed it this way, "As a counselor, I was greatly impressed and moved by the fact that race was forgotten and denominational ties made no difference as far as who counseled whom. Truly, it was a genuine ecumenical experience which I would not likely have had—nor would I have known about it—just by being in the audience as a listener. Whenever anyone speaks of church ecumenicity as a goal set by those in leadership positions, I wonder if it could ever result in anything as genuinely real as the Crusade. I saw with my own eyes, and now know in my own heart, that true oneness can come only when it springs from the changed hearts of those born of God."

The 1982 New England Crusade brought the same results. Milton Noble, registrar at Brown University and chairman of the Providence Crusade rally, said, "This is the first time we have ever had anything in Rhode Island that would bring 200 churches together."[3] An Evangelical Covenant Church pastor, the Reverend Norm Swenson, speaking about the Hartford Crusade rally, said that one of the most important outcomes of the Crusade is that kind of cooperation and mutual support built among churches. He continued, "[Pastors] are learning to trust one another and to work in harmony instead of competition."[4] Dr. Charles E. Hendricks, pastor of Boston's Tremont Temple Baptist Church, observed, "This is a phenomenon. Churches are uniting in an effort the likes of which I have never seen in New England. There is a spirit of unity. Billy Graham is here with an unadulterated purpose in mind—he is here to declare the Gospel. I think that is what draws people together. I hope to see a great many people integrated into the fellowship of the church. I believe that will happen if we take it seriously. It will be up to us."[5]

Emphasis on Evangelism

Prayer, witnessing, and evangelism have an effect on local churches and on the entire community that cannot be measured by Crusade meeting statistics. Following a Crusade in his city, a Reformed Church pastor wrote, "The Billy Graham Crusade gave a tremendous boost to the spiritual life of our church. More than sixty persons were referred to us, with whom we are now continuing our efforts for Christian nurture. We find in visiting within the community that there are many who have opened their minds to the Gospel. It is easier now to get a hearing about the things of Christ. Several entire families have come into the church seeking the way of salvation. Two home prayer groups are being continued, and neighbors are being invited to these. In addition, I have heard several pastors remark that the Crusade brought new vitality to their ministry and emphasized the great essentials of the Gospel."

Dr. Tom Phillips' dissertation pointed out that this emphasis on evangelism results in a new motivation to personal evangelism, especially as a result of the Christian Life and Witness Class training. It also encourages churches to engage actively in programs of outreach.

Noel Krogman, who is an attorney for the U.S. Navy and the evangelism chairman at his church in Newport, Rhode Island, affirmed that the Crusade impact is more than new decisions for Christ. According to Krogman, "Lots of people were involved in training. It has brought an awareness of local evangelism and of one-to-one evangelism." Krogman, who has heard many people say that they feel more prepared to share their faith, stated, "The impact is more than just on the unsaved—the only way to reach them is through the people in the church. More trained and confident Christians will aid this process."[6]

The results during the Crusade meetings tend to set up a chain reaction afterward. A New England Assembly of God pastor identified the Crusade as the major reason for growth in his congregation. He pointed out that at least thirty people have started attending church since the April meetings, yet only three of them came to faith during the Crusade. He said, "As a result of these three, we have gained at least thirty more."[7]

Often what has been sown at the Crusade services is reaped afterward through the local churches. Following the 1954 Billy Graham Crusade at Harringay Arena in London, England, the *British Weekly* polled a cross-section of British clergy of all denominations. As a result of that poll, they reported, ". . . in the months after the 1954 Crusade the number of converts continued to increase. Many people, exposed to Billy Graham's message but undecided at the time, 'moved slowly and thoughtfully to the Christian faith over a period of months.' "[8] It appears that a Crusade has a ripple effect that goes far beyond the initial splash!

Spiritual Renewal

Ministers have often commented that a renewed and rededicated laity were a direct result of their involvement in a Crusade. The statistics from the Firebaugh survey in the Pacific Northwest Crusade indicate that three out of four lay leaders felt the Crusade was an effective spiritual renewal effort for the local church. Also, six out of ten saw the Crusade as helping the local congregations prepare for the discipling of new Christians.

After a Crusade in his city an Albuquerque, New

Mexico, minister affirmed this benefit, "Even beyond the number of families and individuals I have received into membership as a result of the Crusade, the greatest blessing for my church has been spiritual motivation. My people have not been the same! Board members have returned to positions of leadership with deeper joy and clearer vision. Teachers feel more qualified and seem more enthused. Choir members sing with added joy. Undoubtedly my people feel that they have a new pastor and staff also."[9]

A Presbyterian minister from New England agreed that the Crusade has an awakening effect. He said, "The stirring up of people is part of the fruitfulness of the years to come." Pointing out that the responsibility now rests with the churches, he added, "It is not Billy Graham's responsibility to keep people fired up—he acted as a catalyst. Now the churches need to continue what he started."[10]

This renewal touches not only the church but individuals as well. Dr. Glenn Firebaugh's survey of the inquirers from the Pacific Northwest Crusade revealed several factors that confirmed personal spiritual renewal:

1. The number of inquirers who read their Bible every day has tripled since the Crusade;
2. The number of those who attend church several times a week has nearly doubled since the Crusade;
3. The number of those who pray every day has increased by 40 percent since the Crusade;
4. The number of those who attend Bible studies at least once a month has increased by one-third since the Crusade.

Referring to these results, Dr. Lewis Drummond stated, "This kind of individual renewal makes for church renewal. Laymen being motivated to Christian service is another positive spinoff."[11]

New Additions to the Church

Crusade activities across the six-state New England region reported a response of nearly 20,000 inquirers. Most of these inquirers were referred back to local churches. Grace Chapel of Lexington, Massachusetts, reported receiving 220 referrals. After the Crusade Quidnessett Baptist Church in North Kingston, Rhode Island, counted 100 people involved in nurture groups—including 52 first-time commitments. Faith Christian Center in Bedford, New Hampshire, received 130 referrals. Although referrals do not always equal new additions to the church, there is evidence that many churches in New England benefited numerically from the Crusade.

Crusade evangelism is sometimes challenged on the grounds that it does not result in immediate church growth. In dealing with the "presupposition that mass evangelism which does not result in immediate church growth is not effective evangelism," Dr. Drummond replied, "Three things should be said at the outset concerning this . . . criticism. First, an immediate growth goal criterion of success is really no more than a presupposition. It presupposes all evangelistic endeavor must result in *immediate* local church growth if it is worthy. But such a criterion of success is not an established, incontestable 'fact' that can be justified historically or scripturally. It is a presupposition. Local church growth is vital and a long-term objective; but all evangelistic activity need not *necessarily* result in *immediate* local church growth. Most Christians have done personal witnessing that did not result in *immediate* church growth. That is hardly an argument to make us stop sharing the faith. It is hard to justify 'immediate church growth' as the bottom line of any evangelistic methodology. . . .

"Second, the presupposition seems to imply that, unless a church expects to receive an immediate influx of new members as a result of a Crusade, it should not participate. That also is somewhat dubious. . . .

"Finally, the 'immediate growth' criticism rather tacitly assumes that a Graham Crusade does not result in local church growth in any significant way at any time. To this point no substantial evidence has been published that such is the case. In fact, a quite convincing argument can be made to the contrary."[12]

The average pastor values not only new additions to the church, but also the reactivation of people on church rolls who are currently inactive. Names on a roll and occasional appearances in a pew do not constitute a real benefit to the work and mission of the church. A new commitment to Christ and His Church is considered beneficial regardless of whether or not it means a "new addition" to the rolls. Even the most conservative interpretation of data from the Firebaugh survey indicates that 16 percent of the inquirers who came forward in the Pacific Northwest Crusade were *new additions* to the church rolls. Church attendance would be a somewhat higher figure due to the reactivation of existing church members. Significantly, these results occurred during a year when church membership for the twelve largest U.S. denominations in the Seattle/Tacoma area actually declined by three-tenths of one percent.

Dr. Drummond attempts to put this in perspective in his article which compares the Seattle Crusade inquirer response to that of the average church. He wrote, "Consider a typical local church with 300 in attendance. For this church to experience comparable results [to the Crusade] would require approximately twelve public commitments (four for salvation) at *each* preaching service. Two of these would actually become church members. Surely any pastor would be thrilled to gain two new church members for every 300 attending each preaching service."[13]

A Crusade in Cincinnati in the fall of 1977 recorded

160,572 in attendance with 7,075 inquirers. A post-Crusade telephone survey of these inquirers was conducted five weeks after the effort. In response to the question, "Are you attending church regularly?" 83 percent answered "yes" and 17 percent answered "no." Of those answering "no," 47 percent indicated a desire and plan to attend more regularly; and 42 percent requested and were given help in their church relationship. The Cincinnati statistics indicate that a high percentage of the inquirers were attending a church, and half of the remainder wanted to be related to a local church. This kind of church attendance undoubtedly has an impact on local church growth.

The minister of a 1,000-member Presbyterian church inquired about another Crusade in his city ten years after the first one. His reason for a repeat venture was that the greatest growth in his church had occurred in the three to four years after the first Crusade. He concluded that "a crusade does something for our churches which we cannot seem to do for ourselves."

Awareness of Church and Community Needs

One of the important by-products of spiritual renewal among Christians is a new sensitivity to the needs of their Christian brothers and sisters and the needs of others in the community. Following the October, 1977, Crusade meetings in Cincinnati, Ohio, an offering was received to help meet the needs in India where Billy Graham was scheduled to hold four Good News Festivals after the October meetings in Cincinnati. Providentially, this money was available to help rebuild a whole village that was devastated by the typhoon sweeping over the Andhra Pradesh area the next month, November.

In New England a Love-in-Action committee was formed to channel the people's renewed motivation toward community needs. Love-in-Action was designed to mobilize concerned Christians, especially those supporting the 1982 Billy Graham Crusade in Boston. According to Love-in-Action planners, the primary strategy was to link inner-city ministries with suburban churches to help meet human needs in Boston. Through conversation with one another, Bible study, and prayer, Love-in-Action participants opened themselves to what God was calling them to do in witness and service. The 1986 Washington, D.C., Crusade featured a strong Love-in-Action emphasis with public statements by Billy Graham about the Christian social responsibility. Dr. Graham's personal visits to food distribution, housing and job-training programs called attention to the needs of the city, and church leaders met to focus the resources of the Christian community on these needs. In addition, 16,000 pounds of food were collected at the Crusade site to be distributed through local church agencies to people in need. Council of Churches Executive Director Dr. Ernest R. Gibson observed, "The Love-in-Action Committee provides the Billy Graham Crusade with a balance between evangelism and action. It allows the participants in the Crusade to direct the Crusade unity among churches, its energy and momentum, to meet the personal and social needs of people in the area where the Crusade is being held. This practical outpouring of Christian love of which Dr. Graham preaches is an invaluable witness to the integrity and sensitivity of Dr. Graham and the Crusade to the needs of the whole person."

Bishop George W. Bashore, resident bishop of the United Methodist Church in the Boston area and chairman of the Crusade Advisory Committee, commented, "I think the Crusade has given a whole new impetus and encouragement to those of us hoping for renewal in the churches of New England. . . . I particularly like the fact that bridges are being built between personal piety and the need to confront racism, anti-Semitism, and other problems. I also see bridges being built across some of our theological differences. People are coming together, knowing there is a desperate need for spiritual renewal in New England."[14]

Episcopal clergyman, Dr. Charles L. Glenn, who serves as director of the Bureau of Equal Educational Opportunity, Massachusetts Department of Education in Boston, said one evening as he stood near the Crusade platform watching the counselors and inquirers, "It is amazing to see this kind of response in the Boston area, because we are so used to seeing churches being dead or committed only to social causes. But the Gospel is both proclamation and action. This Crusade is bringing these together in an exciting way."[15]

Emphasis on Prayer

Ministers often express their appreciation for the emphasis on prayer in these Crusades. The priority placed on prayer validates the biblical principle that evangelism is not built around personalities, publicity, or programs but it happens by the power of the Holy Spirit working through people. Dependence on prayer and the answers to prayer throughout a Crusade become "Exhibit A" of the scriptural pattern for doing God's work. It also brings new enthusiasm to church members.

Following a Crusade in his city, the minister of a Las Vegas church commented, "We have fifty people in our church who now understand the meaning and value of prayer, and this is making a difference in the spiritual life of our congregation." A pastor from Spokane, Washington, wrote, "In the wake of the Billy Graham Crusade here we have seen a 50 percent increase in Sunday school and a similar increase in worship." After suggesting several factors for this growth, he concluded, "Most of all, one cannot ignore the power of concerted prayer that paved the way for all the rest."

Relating to continuing blessings after a Crusade in his city, a Mississippi pastor wrote, "The greatest thing is a new realization of the importance of prayer. We had an all-night prayer meeting which was a real blessing. We are building a prayer chain of people who will pray during a particular hour each week. We now close our midweek prayer meeting in small groups of four to six people so that everyone can pray."[16] In some cities prayer groups that started during Crusade preparations have continued for years afterward, bringing great blessing to local congregations and to outreach activities in those cities.

Why Churches Reap Results

Following the New England Crusade, a pastor wrote, "As a result of the Crusade, we received but one referral, that of a young man from our church who went forward at one of the meetings. Why, out of all of these decisions and referrals, did we receive only one?" In almost every city at least one pastor will raise this same issue. Dr. Robert O. Ferm, long-time associate of Mr. Graham who has visited thousands of pastors all over the world, answers these questions by asking two of his own: (1) How many of your people were involved in the Crusade preparations? and (2) How many unchurched persons did your members actually bring to the Crusade services? Ferm commented that the answer to these questions is almost always, "Few or none at all." We reap what we sow. The key to additions from a Crusade is *involvement* in the preparations, and *inviting*, yes, bringing the unchurched to the services!

Are the Unchurched Reached?

Another criticism of Crusade results is that very few unchurched persons are reached through the meetings. Dr. Ferm has done extensive research that speaks to that issue. Ferm surveyed 14,000 inquirers from four continents several years after their decision and learned that 46 percent had been unchurched prior to the Crusade, while 54 percent had been affiliated with a church in various degrees. Ferm's research also showed that those responding represented a cross-section of society. Describing that cross-section, Leighton Ford, in his book *The Christian Persuader*, wrote, "It was found that out of every thousand inquirers who [came] forward, one was a lawyer, two were university professors, two high school teachers, two doctors, ten men in other professions, ten businessmen, twenty career women, fifty children, 100 laboring men, 200 housewives, and 600 students. (There was also half a policeman!)"[17]

Assessing the Results

Billy Graham has said that the results of a Crusade cannot be adequately assessed until five to ten years afterward. Although it is too early to assess in depth the results of the 1982 New England meetings, it is possible to take a long-term look because of two previous New England Crusades in 1950 and 1964.

Executive director of the Evangelistic Association of New England, Donald Gill, commented on this long-term result, "Throughout the Crusade organization in New England, there were scores and scores of individuals who had met Christ in earlier Crusades. It takes time, of course, to see such results, but we have faith that the Lord will allow similar leadership to emerge from those who came to faith in Christ during the 1982 Crusade."

Allan Emery, Jr., a respected Christian businessman and chairman of both the 1950 and 1964 New England Crusades, wrote, "In both Crusades the ministers themselves were perhaps the most altered. I think that probably the greatest impact was the commitment that ministers made—not only to a saving faith, but also to the inerrant Word of God. When Billy started preaching 'the Bible says . . . ,' ministers saw that there was real authority in this. Instead of just quoting the verse, clergy preached the verse. As a result, there is now an earnestness in the pulpits, a desire for presenting the Gospel so as to evoke decisions."

Unlike the statistics in 1950 when evangelical churches were a small minority in New England, a survey published in 1982 by the Evangelistic Association of New England indicates that church attendance in evangelical and conservative churches is equal to or greater than those who would classify themselves as nonevangelical. The Providence *Journal Bulletin* reported, "More than half the Protestants attending church in any given week go to . . . an evangelical church."

London, England

What is true of the Crusade meetings in New England is true of Crusades across the world. In 1954 Billy Graham spent three months at London's Harringay Arena and that Crusade recorded some 38,000 decisions for Christ. Stanley High, writing for *Reader's Digest* on the subject, "Do Billy Graham's Crusades Have a Lasting Effect?" went back to England in 1955 to survey the impact of those meetings. According to High, the interdenominational church paper, *The British Weekly*, surveyed a cross section of the British clergy and "found that of the outsiders (neither church members nor regular churchgoers) converted at Harringay, 64 percent 'are still attending church and taking part in church life regularly.' "[18] He reported, "At All Souls Church (Langham Place) in London the Rev. John R. W. Stott preaches to one of England's largest Anglican congregations. Of 200 converts in his church, 'few have failed to continue to grow in faith.' Sixty converts were received at Westminster Central Hall, largest Methodist Church in Great Britain. All but six of them are still full-fledged members of the church, increasingly active in its work."[19]

Sydney, Australia

What is true of New England and England is also true of Sydney, Australia, where Billy Graham held a Crusade in 1959. Bishop A. Jack Dain, of the Anglican Church of New South Wales, reported that between 1959 and 1968 approximately 50 percent of all the ministerial students attending Moore Theological College in Sydney had been converted in the previous Graham meetings. It was this fact, as much as any other, that caused the Primate of Australia, Archbishop Sir Marcus Loane, who had served as chairman of Counseling and Follow-Up during the 1959 meetings, to invite Billy Graham back to Sydney for a three-week Crusade in 1979. Some 491,000 persons attended the meetings, with 22,500 recording their decisions for Christ. According to Bishop Dain, 11,000 to 12,000 of these were Anglicans. A thorough survey by the diocese revealed that 72.6 percent of these were in full church membership one year later, not including those who had moved away from the city and could not be counted. Bishop Dain went on to state that although hard data were not available on all inquirers, he reliably estimates that 70 percent of the 22,500 had been brought into the life of the church and were continuing in their commitment to Christ.

In light of these testimonies and other statistical evidence, we can answer the question, "Do the results last?" with an inarguable "YES!"

Perhaps the benefits and blessings of a Crusade are best summed up by the testimony of Dr. Richard Anderson, pastor of First Baptist Church in Indianapolis, Indiana. During the Indianapolis Crusade in the spring of 1980, he said from the Crusade platform, "Last Sunday was my thirtieth spiritual birthday. Thirty years ago as a rebellious teenager, without any goals in my life and with a great emptiness in my heart, I reluctantly accepted an invitation from my father to attend a Billy Graham rally on Old Boston Common.

"There were more than 50,000 people present that afternoon. Most of us had to stand, and we could hardly move in the huge crowd. As Billy started to speak, I felt my heart begin to open to the message of God's redeeming love in Christ Jesus. And it was like water to a thirsty, dying man. At the invitation the crowd was too large for anyone to go forward. So we were asked to raise our hand if we wanted to pray that our sins would be forgiven, and if we wanted peace in our hearts. With apprehension and great fear, I timidly raised my hand. Christ did come in, and my emptiness was filled with His presence.

"My life changed that day. I went home and began to read the Bible. I read it through in less than a year. I started attending church. As often as the doors of the church were open, I was there. When I returned to high school, I completed subjects that I had failed during my rebellion. Several years later I enrolled in college; and after that, in seminary. For the past thirty years, I've been an ambassador for Christ—a preacher of the saving grace of Jesus Christ. And, during these years, it has been my privilege to see many come to know Him as personal Savior, to grow in the faith, and to dedicate their lives to Christian ministry.

"Last Sunday, on the thirtieth anniversary of my Christian birth, I had the privilege of sitting on this platform. But, you know, that wasn't my greatest privilege that day. As the invitation was given, from up in the stands my youngest child, the last one of our children to receive Jesus Christ, got out of her seat, walked down the aisle, and gave her life to Jesus Christ. Now our whole family is in the hands of the Lord. How I praise Him for that! My song of praise is this, 'To God be the glory, great things He has done.' "

In Reveiw:

1. Ministers point to seven primary benefits from Crusade evangelism:
   A. The training of laity which accrues to the local church.
   B. The unifying of Christians across denominational lines.
   C. The increased emphasis on witness and evangelism.
   D. The spiritual renewal of the laity and thus the church.
   E. The new additions to the church.
   F. A new sensitivity to church and community needs.
   G. A new appreciation for the power of prayer.
2. Surveys of thousands of inquirers on several continents during more than a decade reveal that an amazingly high proportion are still actively involved in the life of the church years later. When the Holy Spirit does the work, the results do last!

10
Potential:
These Principles
Can Work for You

The fulfillment of the Great Commission has obviously not been delegated to Crusade evangelism in general or Billy Graham Crusades in particular, although both have a part in the total task of world evangelization. God's strategy is much broader and more universally applicable than one person, method, or program. It is for that reason this book does not elaborate on programs or procedures, but rather seeks to identify the biblical principles behind them.

These principles for effective evangelism are applicable throughout the life of Christ's Church. Only the magnitude, context, or form is changed to fit the specific resources and opportunity. The mission remains constant: "Go and make disciples." Thus, these principles apply to single church, small group, neighborhood, visitation, and personal evangelism, among other methods.

Just as Crusade evangelism mobilizes the resources of many local congregations for the purpose of proclaiming the Gospel to a whole city or metropolitan area, so each local congregation mobilizes its people to fulfill the Great Commission in its sphere of influence. Local churches are motivated to evangelism through a sincere acceptance of Christ's mandate for His Church.

The Church Should Grow

God's strategy for achieving world evangelization is simple, and yet often dimly perceived. It is for the church to grow. The Church, Christ's Body, is primarily a living organism and only secondarily an organization. All living organisms grow. Growth is a natural and spontaneous expression of life. The church is to be the embodiment of spiritual life, and one of the signs of that life is growth.

The Bible identifies two kinds of growth for the church: reproduction and maturity. Reproductive, or numerical, growth is illustrated for us throughout the book of Acts by such passages as: "The same day there were added unto them about three thousand souls" (Acts 2:41, KJV); "The Lord added to the church daily such as should be saved" (Acts 2:47, KJV); "The word of God increased; and the number of the disciples multiplied in Jerusalem greatly" (Acts 6:7, KJV). Growth in maturity refers to spiritual depth and strength in the church as it develops internally. Paul prayed for the Colossian church that it "might be filled with the knowledge of his will, . . . being fruitful in every good work" (Colossians 1:9-10, KJV). Both external growth (quantitative) and internal growth (qualitative) are essential for a healthy church.

Although we expect the Church to grow, not all churches do grow. In recent years a number of the traditional Protestant denominations have been alarmed over not only the decline in growth, but also a significant loss of members. This has caused a re-evaluation of priorities and a re-emphasis on evangelism in a number of cases. But lack of growth is not limited just to those of the more "liberal" tradition. Conservative churches, which generally have shown growth, can also lose the balance between quantitative and qualitative growth. Such a church which had experienced little growth over the last decade was characterized by one interested observer as "over fed and under exercised." Just as our physical body requires exercise to maintain its vitality and muscle tone, so does the spiritual body—the church. The church must exercise in proper balance the gifts given to it in order that the body may be healthy and, as a result, continue to grow.

Setting Goals for Growth

In recent years church growth specialists have provided helpful insights about why churches do or do not grow. Dr. C. Peter Wagner, professor of church growth at Fuller Theological Seminary, pointed out that there are two factors common to churches that grow:

1. They set goals for growth. That is, they believe the church should grow; they plan to grow, and they expect to grow!
2. They assimilate into the church new persons who are brought into it. New attenders do not simply enter by the front door and then leave by the back door. Rather, they become active members of the congregation.[1]

Dr. O. D. Emery, general secretary of church education in the Wesleyan church, concluded from a survey of fifty growing churches within his denomination, "A growing congregation understands that God expects their church to reach the lost with the Gospel." He went on to say, "We desperately need a growth conscience. We need to feel alarmed and uneasy over lack of fruit in spiritual harvest." And he concluded that "growing churches are churches with an expectancy, an anticipation, an attitude of excitement for what God is doing through their church."[2]

Goals are essential for growth. It has been said, "If we aim at nothing, we are bound to hit it." But if we set goals, we are likely to reach and even exceed them.

Wagner likened establishing goals to an act of faith:

"Goal setting is a modern equivalent to the biblical concept of faith. 'Without faith it is impossible to please [God]' (Hebrews 11:6, KJV). What is faith? 'Faith is the substance of things hoped for' (Hebrews 11:1, KJV). Things hoped for are, of course, all future. For reasons I do not fully understand, some power is released through setting positive goals that otherwise remain dormant. But although I cannot explain it as well as I wish I could, it is a biblical principle that God seems to honor and that has been demonstrated in numerous body evangelism efforts and elsewhere. Paul Yonggi Cho, pastor of the world's largest church in Seoul, Korea, put it this way: 'The number one requirement for having real church growth—unlimited church growth—is to set goals.' I do not believe that this dynamic can be overstressed."[3]

Goals for growth mean goals to "make disciples" in obedience to Christ's mandate. The qualitative goals of spiritual maturity, though important to the life and health of the church, are not enough to fulfill this mandate. There must also be quantitative goals. The church needs to set numerical goals for outreach and new additions to the "community of faith."

A passion for outreach and a plan for outreach are essential for growth. Lyle Schaller, writing from his experience of twenty years, researching growing congregations, reported that one characteristic which nearly all growing congregations have in common is "an evangelistic emphasis" which "has its most important expression in laypersons."[4] That same conclusion was reached by Dr. O. D. Emery, who wrote, "In a growing church the method is never considered as important as the task. Under God, a healthy church possesses a growth conscience which prompts it to 'outreach at all costs' and then finds the methods that will be most successful. A growing church sees itself as responsible to God for the multitudes of lost people around it—and responsible for finding appropriate methods to reach these people."[5]

A Strategy for Growth

Goals alone are not enough. Having defined our goals, we must choose a strategy to reach those goals. The biblical strategy given to us by Jesus is that one sows, another reaps, and all rejoice together in the "gathered fruit" (John 4:35-37). Every true believer has the responsibility to be "light" and "salt" within the web of relationships that surrounds his life. Through his loving acts he cultivates the soil of an unbeliever's heart, preparing it to receive the "good seed." Then through his living witness he sows the Word of God in that life, which is open to receive that witness.

But that is only half of the strategy. After the sowing must come that reaping. So the church needs to exercise the "gift of an evangelist" in order to reap what has been sown. This truth was clearly demonstrated to my wife and me several years ago. We had witnessed to Bill, a young man who did some landscaping around our home. But he did not make a commitment to Christ. However, later when Billy Graham's Associate Evangelist, Dr. Ralph Bell, came to our church for evangelistic meetings, we invited Bill to attend. He responded to the message and made his commitment to Christ. We had cultivated, sown, and watered, but it was when the gift of an evangelist was exercised that God brought the increase.

The Gift of an Evangelist

Peter Wagner stated, "It is obvious that the one gift above all others necessary for church growth is the gift of evangelist."[6] The gift of an evangelist is that

special ability God gives to some members of the Body
of Christ which enables them to share clearly the Gospel with unbelievers so that they will commit their
lives to Christ. While affirming that the evangelist's
gift is primary, Wagner pointed out the need for the
other gifts of the Body in spiritual reproduction. "But
the finest gift of an evangelist in Christendom will not
help churches to grow if the other members of the
Body, the secondary organs for church growth, are
not also functioning in a healthy manner."[7]

Wagner further pointed out that "the average
Christian church can realistically expect that approximately 10 percent of its active adult members will
have been given the gift of evangelist."[8] Does this
make the other 90 percent who are not given that gift
ineffective or unimportant in the church's mission of
evangelism? Hardly! Their role is all important in cultivating, sowing, and watering in order to ensure a
harvest. A wheat farmer in the Pacific Northwest
shared with me that 80 to 90 percent of his efforts are
spent in preparing the harvest, and only about 10 percent in the actual reaping process. And he reaps the
entire harvest with only one piece of equipment.

So it is in the church. Not every Christian is gifted
as an evangelist, but every Christian can be, and is, a
witness. Evangelist Leighton Ford wrote that a danger
in emphasizing spiritual gifts is that people may become so specialized they will say, "Well, I don't share
my faith because that is not my gift." Ford, who ad-
mitted that God makes certain people evangelists
through spiritual gifts, also said, "We must not use
the teaching of spiritual gifts as a cop-out to avoid our
responsibility to share Christ with others. You may
not be called as an evangelist, but you and every
Christian, by an attitude of love, by compassionate
concern, and by well-chosen words, can have the
privilege to lead others . . . toward Jesus Christ."[9]
Every Christian can and should seek to lead others to faith

in Christ, even though this may not be his primary gift.

David Hubbard, president of Fuller Seminary, affirms that truth in this way, "Not all of us have the gift of evangelism. I admire people who can lead others to Jesus Christ right on the spot, who have the ability to turn every conversation into an occasion for sharing God's plan of salvation. I am not one of those, but I have a story to share—and so do you. I have a relationship with Christ that I can describe—and so do you. Evangelism will best take place when all of God's people have learned to express their winsome witness."[10] The role and responsibility of each Christian in the process of evangelizing should be affirmed and encouraged.

Part of that encouragement is insuring that both sides of Christ's strategy are kept in balance—the sowing and the reaping. Without adequate sowing, those who have been gifted in reaping will experience frustration and a meager harvest. Conversely, challenging the 90 percent to sow generously to the world of relationships around their lives, without providing trained people to reap and opportunities for reaping, will frustrate the sowers. The church must keep both in balance in its emphasis and planning.

It is commonly assumed that the gift of an evangelist, as bestowed by the Holy Spirit, will be exercised by a person—particularly someone who is adept at personal soul winning or public proclamation of the Gospel. However, Scripture also supports the concept that persons who are primarily gifted in other ways may from time to time exercise this gift also, but perhaps in a more limited way. Timothy, whose gift seems to be largely that of a pastor-teacher, was admonished to "do the work of an evangelist" (2 Timothy 4:5, KJV). This also occurs when the pastor, on occasion, preaches an evangelistic sermon; a Sunday school teacher armed with an appropriate lesson invites decision from class members; the camp counselor looks for God's moment in the life of a camper; and so on.

The gift of an evangelist is also available to the church in many media forms—printed materials, audio and video tapes, film strips, films, radio, TV. Gifted persons have merely transferred the evangelistic appeal to a different form of communication to extend their ministry.

"Doing the work of an evangelist" is not confined to the vocational evangelist alone of which Scripture gives us only one example (Acts 8:5–40; 21:8).

Thank God for those who are gifted and called proclaimers. But the work of reaping is not limited to their numbers or their availability. Rather, the "gift of an evangelist" can be made available to the local congregation through a wide variety of methods and persons. These include, among other methods, pastoral preaching, Sunday school teaching and special programs, visitation evangelism, daily vacation Bible school, camps, retreats, evangelistic dinners and breakfasts, special musical programs, films, and local church evangelistic Crusades. The American Festival of Evangelism held in July, 1980, offered workshops on some 200 of the finest methods of equipping, evangelizing, and discipling available to the church today. An invaluable collection of notebooks, with brief summaries of each of these methods, is available as a resource to the local church. (See Appendix G: Local Congregation Resources.)

No one method of evangelism is applicable to every congregation and every situation. That is why this book has emphasized principles and then illustrated them with methods. Many of these same principles apply whether the evangelism is one-to-one, neighborhood Bible studies, local church events, or citywide Crusades. Each church must choose methods that fit its congregation and its potential mission field. The choice of those methods and their application can best be done in light of these biblical principles for effective evangelism.

The Need for Application

The late Joe Blinco, a former BGEA associate evangelist, told of an experience of witnessing to Christ with a friend one day in Hyde Park, London. His friend was preaching the Gospel to a half-interested and skeptical audience. As he courageously expounded the good news, telling how it can change individuals, society, and the world, a dirty, unkempt man cynically interrupted with the question, "If the Gospel's as good as you say it is, how come it's been around for 2,000 years and the world's still in the mess it's in?" Joe recounts that his friend, with great presence of mind, answered by saying, "Water has been around for 10,000 years and soap for 5,000 years, but look at the back of your neck." Soap and water were both *available* and *able* to meet the man's need; *the problem was lack of application!*

For the church, application begins with establishing goals for outreach and growth. Ask God to reveal to you His goals and grant you faith to commit yourselves as a body of believers to them. Make sure they are SMART goals:

> Specific
> Measurable
> Achievable
> Reviewable
> Time-defined

You do not really set a goal unless you believe with God's help you can attain it and are committed to reaching it. Some resources for goal-setting and church growth are provided in the appendix. (See Appendix G: Local Congregation Resources.)

Reaching those goals requires an evangelistic strategy: Christians sowing by their loving witness to those around them and the church offering opportunities for reaping. The choice of methods for reaping and the application of those methods needs to be made in light of biblical principles of evangelism. This book seeks to identify some of those principles in order to help the Church fulfill the Great Commission.

In Review:

1. In fulfilling the Great Commission, the Church is expected to grow, both quantitatively and qualitatively.
2. Setting numerical goals is an important part of quantitative growth.
3. The strategy for these goals requires a proper balance between sowing and reaping.
4. Choosing methods to achieve these goals, and especially for reaping, should be done in light of biblical principles.

11

Person:

The Servant God Uses

E.M. Bounds has observed, "The church is looking for better methods; God is looking for better men." For evangelism to be effective it is important that we define the purpose, explain the biblical principles, clarify the process, and delineate the procedures. These are crucial to apply efficiently the energies and abilities of people who are committed to fulfilling the Great Commission. But, even more important than the methods of evangelism are the men and women in leadership. This includes both the clergy who lead their churches, and the laity who carry out the task. They must be persons who are committed to be used of God, for God has chosen to work through people just like you and me. It is *people* who commit to a purpose, apply principles, and implement procedures.

The prophet Ezekiel pointed this out when he prophesied for the Lord, "I sought for a man among them, that should make up the hedge, and stand in the gap before me for the land, that I should not destroy it: but I found none. Therefore have I poured out mine indignation upon them; I have consumed them with the fire of my wrath: their own way have I recompensed upon their heads, saith the Lord God" (Ezekiel 22:30–31, KJV). God brought judgment upon the people partially because of the failure of their religious leaders. He had looked for a man, a prophet, who would stand among them, and He could find none. What kind of man or woman should one be in order to be used of God?

Billy Graham has often spoken to evangelists, pastors, seminary students, and leaders in world evangelism on this topic. In his messages Graham emphasizes seven credentials of the servant whom God uses:

First, the servant of God must be sure he has had a personal experience with Jesus Christ. John Wesley said, "What a dreadful thing it would be for me if I should be ignorant of the power of the truth which I am preparing to proclaim." Wesley had been a missionary to Georgia, but something was missing in his life. He left Georgia, writing in his journal, "I went to America to convert the heathen but, oh, who will convert me?" Then after he had been to the historic Aldersgate meeting, he described the change that God worked in his life through faith in Christ. He said, "I felt my heart strangely warmed. I felt I did trust in Christ and Christ alone for my salvation; and an assurance was given to me that He had taken away my sins, even mine, and saved me from the law of sin and death." Has that happened to you? Richard Baxter said, "God never saved any man for being a preacher." Make sure that you know Jesus Christ personally. Don't be too proud to say, "Oh, God, I've preached to others but I myself am still a sinner in need of a Savior." We must be absolutely convinced of our own salvation before we can communicate that hope and assurance to others. It's a principle. The ancient rabbis used to say, "First be trained thyself and then adorn thy brother. The hand that means to make another clean must not itself be dirty."

Second, the servant of God must be sure that he has a call from God. Have you been called of God to be where you are? Jeremiah said, "But his word was in mine heart as a burning fire shut up in my bones" (Jeremiah

20:9, KJV). Do you sense this burning within your bones? Too many seminary students in America today are going into the ministry as a profession, just as one would train to become a doctor or a lawyer or something else, never having been called of God. The ministry must be a call, not just a profession. The early apostles said, "For we cannot but speak the things which we have seen and heard" (Acts 4:20, KJV). Paul said, "For necessity is laid upon me; yea, woe is unto me, if I preach not the gospel!" (1 Corinthians 9:16, KJV). Paul had to do it, because God had called him and he could do nothing else. Lloyd Ogilvie said, "If we have a ministry only because we are in the ministry, then we do not have an authentic ministry." The ministry is a calling. Are you sure that God has called you? The person who has been called by God and knows it will be used of God.

Third, the servant of God must have a systematic devotional life. There is no substitute for a daily, disciplined meeting with God through His Word and in prayer. Job said, "I have esteemed the words of his mouth more than my necessary food" (Job 23:12, KJV). Is that true for you? In a survey taken at a large theological seminary in the United States, 93 percent of those students studying for the ministry said, "I have no devotional life." I can tell you they are going to be powerless preachers. That's where your power comes from, in your closet when you are alone with God—in the study of the Word and in prayer. In my years of ministry I have never met an effective Christian who did not have a regular devotional life.

Fourth, the servant of God must be a person of prayer. Pray without ceasing. We need to be constantly praying. James said, "The effectual fervent prayer of a righteous man availeth much" (James 5:16, KJV). One hundred years ago a British theologian said, "All our libraries and studies are mere emptiness compared to our closets." Somebody said, "Beware of the barrenness of a busy life." How busy we can be in the ministry today!

Are you a man or a woman of prayer? In our work as a pastor or teacher or professor or evangelist, we can get terribly professional. We have to have an experience that will make us weep over souls. John Vassar, of Boston, the great soul-winner, knocked on the door of a person's home and asked the woman who opened the door if she knew Christ as her Savior. She said, "It's none of your business," and slammed the door in his face. As she watched him out of her window, he stood on the doorstep and wept and wept and wept. The next Sunday she presented herself for church membership. She said it was his tears. Where are our tears for souls today?

Fifth, the servant of God must be Spirit-filled. Scripture commands us to be filled with the Holy Spirit. The Holy Spirit indwells all of us, but does He fill us all, and is He producing fruit? In some places where you cannot publicly use the gifts of the Spirit, the Holy Spirit can demonstrate the fruit of the Spirit through you. And the firstfruit of the Spirit is love.

In his book titled *The Holy Spirit*, Billy Graham explains that although God gives us the Holy Spirit at conversion, we are commanded to be filled with the Holy Spirit; we are to confess and repent of all known sin, to yield ourselves completely to God, to walk by faith. He wrote, "Each day we should seek to understand more from God's Word. We should pray that God will help us see our sin each day. Each day we should confess and repent. And each day we should submit our wills to His will. We should so walk in faith that He is continually filling us as we submit to Him. Each day we should walk in obedience to His Word.

"Personally I find it helpful to begin each day by silently committing that day into God's hands. I thank Him that I belong to Him, and I thank Him that He knows what the day holds for me. I ask Him to take my life that day and use it for His glory. I ask Him to cleanse me from anything which would hinder His work in my life. And then I step out in faith, knowing that His Holy Spirit is filling me continually as I trust in Him and obey His Word. Sometimes during the day I may not be aware of His presence; sometimes I am. But at the end of the day, I can look back and thank Him, because I see His hand at work. He promised to be with me that day—and He has been!"[1]

Sixth, the servant of God must have a compassionate and sensitive social conscience. There is no way we can fulfill the command of our Lord to be witnesses to Him without having a caring concern for the whole man . . . his spiritual, material, and social needs. Jesus was filled with compassion when He saw the multitudes hungry and sick as well as when He saw them lost as sheep without a shepherd. The world desperately needs to see the love of God as well as to hear it. The mission of the church to the world is twofold: proclamation—*kerygma,* and service—*diakonia.* They go hand in hand, and we ought to set an example by our love, by our compassion, and by helping people who are less fortunate. We are to be calling for peace, for the lifting of oppression throughout the world, and for human rights. I think that is part of our ministry today. And that also will be used of God. As Paul said, "I have become all things to all men" (1 Corinthians 9:22, NIV). Our social concern will be used of God to catch the attention of people who ordinarily might not listen to the Gospel.

Seventh, the servant of God will have a love for his brothers and sisters in the ministry. One of the things that could bring renewal and revival to the world is a new love that crosses all denominational barriers. Jesus said, "A new commandment I give unto you, That ye love one another; as I have loved you, that ye also love one another. By this shall all men know that ye are my disciples, if ye have love one to another" (John 13:34–35, KJV).

Love demonstrates itself in practical ways: Love serves one another. Jesus said, "Whosoever will be chief among you, let him be your servant" (Matthew 20:27, KJV). Our Lord, when He washed the disciples' feet, was our example of service. In love we are patient with one another, courteous to one another. We set an example to each other in our speech, conduct, faith, and purity. In love we forgive one another and are kind and tenderhearted toward one another for Christ's sake. We do not judge one another. We are subject to each other, we edify each other, and we pray for one another.

Billy Graham has preached this message with authority, and audiences have received it readily and thoughtfully. Why? Perhaps the reason is found in the words of Harry Denman, former secretary of evangelism for the United Methodist Church, who said, "You can speak the Gospel, but if you don't live it, you can't preach it." Dr. Harold John Ockenga, referring to his thirty years of association with Billy Graham, has written, "What manner of man have I found? A friend, and much more. One who is the epitome of honesty in his financial dealings; one who is self-denying in his personal affairs, godly in his actions, generous to the poor, compassionate to those who do not know Jesus Christ, truthful in his statements; and above all, faithful to his Lord, to the Gospel, and to the Word of God. Billy Graham is not perfect, and would be the first to say so; after all, only one perfect Man ever walked this earth. But we who are Billy's friends, can say one thing for him: he is the same person in private that he is in public."[2]

Many people have marveled at the way the Billy Graham Team has remained together for more than thirty-five years of ministry. There are two primary reasons for this: First, Team members have been willing to accept their own particular role, and use their gifts to complement each other in order to reach a larger goal. They have not sought each other's role or each other's recognition, but have faithfully fulfilled their own calling. It has truly been a "team" ministry.

Second, they have exercised the qualities of love spoken about by Billy Graham. Mr. Graham himself has been an example of love, kindness, patience, and consideration toward his Team. His example is reflected by Cliff Barrows, who has provided the leaven of a loving spirit in Team relationships, and by George Beverly Shea who is known for his kind and thoughtful ways. This unity does not just happen. It has to be a priority in relationships. Ultimately, as Billy Graham has often said, it can occur only through the enabling and filling of the Holy Spirit.

A life that is committed to Christ and called to follow Him, filled with the Holy Spirit, disciplined through study of the Word and prayer, and willing to serve for Jesus' sake, is a life God can use. Effective evangelism occurs through men and women like that who are willing to serve one another in a spirit of love and cooperation. And they must have one consuming passion: to spread the good news of salvation through Jesus Christ. All other desires are brought into subjection to Jesus Christ for this supreme purpose of making Him known.

In 1867, two young men were talking on a park bench in Dublin, Ireland. One of them, Henry Varley, said, "The world has yet to see what God will do with a man fully consecrated to Him." He didn't say a great man. He didn't say an educated man. He didn't say a rich man. He said someone fully consecrated. The other man meditated on that thought for weeks. It so gripped him that one day he exclaimed, "By the Holy Spirit in me I'll be that man." Historians now say that he touched two continents for Christ. His name was Dwight L. Moody. Are you willing to be totally yielded to God, so that you can be the man or woman God uses?

In Review:

Take spiritual inventory of your own life comparing it with the criteria presented in this chapter:

	Yes	No	Sometimes
1. Are you sure that you know Christ personally?	___	___	___
2. Are you sure of your call from God?	___	___	___
3. Do you have a systematic daily, devotional life?	___	___	___
4. Do you regularly spend time in prayer?	___	___	___
5. Do you know that you are filled with the Holy Spirit?	___	___	___
6. Do you show compassion and concern for the needs of people around you?	___	___	___
7. Do you demonstrate love for brothers and sisters in the ministry?	___	___	___
8. Can it be said of you that you are the same person in private that you are in public?	___	___	___

12

Passion:

The Urgency
to Evangelize

A study of the precedent for modern-day evangelism reveals a history of people who were committed above all else to the Great Commission, "going and making disciples." It is a record of "flaming hearts" who were so motivated to reach lost humanity that they broke, when necessary, with traditions of the past and created new methods to reach the masses of their day. One common ingredient invariably evident in the lives of those past proclaimers of the Gospel who experienced special blessing in their ministry was that paramount essential to all effective evangelism: *A passion for souls!*

The messenger, the methods, and the materials for spreading the Gospel will be only "dry bones" without Holy Spirit-inspired motivation. The content of the message is vital, but a sound message can be possessed by those who are "sound asleep." Knowing the message, the methods, and even the mandate of the Great Commission does not guarantee that one will go . . . or go with compassion . . . or go with enthusiasm . . . or go with urgency! The great need in evangelism today is for the church to recover a passion for souls.

As Leighton Ford so aptly pointed out, "Before

evangelism is a program, it is a passion—a passion of the heart which issues in saving action. Evangelism is the passion of Moses, 'Oh, this people have sinned . . . yet now, if thou wilt forgive their sin—if not, blot me, I pray thee, out of the book which thou hast written.' It is the passion of Paul, 'Woe is me if I preach not the Gospel.' It is the anguished cry of Jesus as He weeps over a doomed city, 'Oh, Jerusalem, how oft would I have gathered thee.'

"Evangelism is the cry of John Knox, 'Give me Scotland or I die,' and of John Wesley, 'The world is my parish.' Evangelism is Henry Martyn landing on the shores of India and crying, 'Here let me burn out for God!' It is David Brainerd coughing up blood from his tubercular lungs as he prays in the snow for the North American Indians. It is George Whitefield crossing the Atlantic thirteen times in a small ship to preach in the American colonies.

"Evangelism is the passion that leads the aristocratic Lady Donnithorne of our own generation to enter the forbidding slums of Hong Kong's 'Walled City' to bring the healing of the Gospel to the pimps and prostitutes, the dope addicts and gamblers. It is Jim Elliot and his young friends staining the sands of a little river in Ecuador with their blood to reach an obscure band of Auca Indians for Christ. It is Paul Carlson leaving his comfortable practice in California for the Congo, there to die with a rebel's bullet through his head."[1]

Dr. Ishaya Audu, a professor from Nigeria, affirmed this truth at the World Congress on Evangelism in Berlin. "Evangelism has all the urgency of the faithful physician when someone is desperately and dangerously ill, of the surgeon when only an emergency operation will save a patient's life, of the fire brigade when someone is trapped inside a burning building, of an army of emancipation hastening to rescue captives held by a cruel tyrant, and of someone who has news too good to keep. It must be told, necessity is laid upon us, cost what it may."[2]

The common motivation in the work of evangelism is in very truth a passion for souls. Methods have changed as society, culture, and technology have changed. But changes should reflect an adaptation of biblical principles for evangelism to contemporary society in order to fulfill effectively the divine purpose.

It is important to note that the methods of Crusade evangelism do not create the evangelist's ministry. Rather, they serve the demand created by a God-anointed ministry. As an evangelist is motivated with a passion for souls and his ministry is blessed with results, the need for better methods is mandated. Billy Graham's 1950 meetings in New England were spontaneous, bordering on revival, and basically unstructured by 1980 standards. As the response to his preaching continued in subsequent Crusades, Mr. Graham felt an ever-deepening conviction that better methods had to be employed, both in preparation and in follow-up. As a result, when he returned to New England in 1964, Crusade preparations were conducted at such depth that the results extended much more deeply into the life of local churches with an impact far beyond the meetings themselves.

"He Was Moved With Compassion"

When we accept Christ's compassion in the work of evangelism, several questions arise. Where does this motivation come from? How do we maintain it? And what do we do when the fire seems to have died down or even gone out?

The primary motive to evangelize comes from our love for Jesus Christ. Jesus said, "If ye love me, keep my commandments" (John 14:15, KJV). And He commanded us to take this good news to the ends of the earth. Billy Graham expressed it this way: "Our chief motive for evangelism is not the world's physical, moral, philosophical, and spiritual needs, as great as they may be. Our primary motivation in evangelism is that we are disciples of the Lord Jesus Christ 'under orders.' We *must* proclaim the Gospel because He has ordered us to do it. Our Lord has commanded us to 'go,' 'to proclaim,' and to 'make disciples,' and that is enough. If we do not evangelize, we will be disobedient to our Lord."[3]

Obedience to Christ means that we must take upon our heart the burden of His heart. Christ's compassion for lost men and women must become our compassion. Compassion is that irrepressible inward desire to reach out and touch someone in need. Our English word "compassion" came from two Latin words: *Com*, meaning together; and *Pati*, meaning to suffer. Compassion means to hurt when you see someone else hurting, or to feel the need of others to the point that it breaks your heart. The Scripture always links compassion with evangelism. Upon seeing the multitudes, Jesus "was moved with compassion . . . because they fainted, and were scattered abroad, as sheep having no shepherd. Then saith he unto his disciples, The harvest truly is plenteous, but the laborers are few" (Matthew 9:36–37, KJV). Christ was moved with compassion as He saw the lostness of mankind. As we share His compassion and obey His commission, our concern for lost mankind is also increased.

The Lostness of Mankind

Man is lost today in this life. He is searching for purpose and peace, security and absolutes. He is in the midst of a feeling of great cosmic loneliness. He fears death. He finds a gnawing in his soul, which he can't seem to satisfy regardless of how much sex, drugs, violence, or entertainment he pours into his life. And so he wanders aimlessly through life trying to find happiness in the pursuit of physical and material gain, all the while not knowing how to deal with the guilt of his life. Man needs Jesus Christ, who can fill that void, forgive his sins, and give direction to his life.

Man is also lost for all eternity. Paul reasoned, "Knowing therefore the terror of the Lord, we persuade men" (2 Corinthians 5:11, KJV). Paul also said that the love of Christ constrains us. On the one hand, Paul was obedient to the call of Christ. On the other, he saw the needs of those around him. This is most clearly expressed when he speaks of his own people saying, "For I could wish that myself were accursed from Christ for my brethren, my kinsmen according to the flesh" (Romans 9:3, KJV). Paul's concern and passion for his lost brethren led him to saying he would be willing to be forever damned if that would save them.

It is only as we see the lostness of mankind that our hearts are infused with compassion for their need. General William Booth, founder of the Salvation Army, once said that he would like to send all of his candidates for officership to hell for twenty-four hours as the chief part of their training. Only thus would they be able to accept the sacrifice required in winning the lost. When William C. Burns, who was instrumental in revival in Robert Murray McCheyne's Scottish parish and later in China, was commencing his ministry, his mother met him in a sordid Glasgow street. Noticing that he was weeping, she asked him, "Why those tears?" He responded, "I am weeping at the sight of the multitudes in the street, so many of whom are passing through life unsaved."

The Motivation to Evangelize

Our motivation to evangelize is twofold: Our obedience to Christ's command and our response to man's need. But how can we maintain that kind of urgency? A passion for souls comes from the Lord Himself. Sometimes it comes at the point of conversion. Most often it comes at the point of our total surrender to Christ and the infilling of the Holy Spirit. After a powerful work of the Holy Spirit in his life, Charles Finney said, "Nay, I found that I was unwilling to do anything else. I had no longer any desire to practice law. . . . I had no disposition to make money. I had no hungering and thirsting after worldly pleasures and amusements in any direction. . . . Nothing, it seemed, could be put into competition with the worth of souls, and no labor . . . could be so sweet . . . as that of holding up Christ to a dying world."[4]

Finney maintained his sense of urgency, not only by his obedience, but by his intense times of prayer. When he went to Boston in 1843, he was warned by Lyman Beecher that this city, the heart of Universalism and Unitarianism, would not respond to his traditional ministry. He answered, "During the winter the Lord gave my own soul a very thorough overhauling and a fresh baptism of His Spirit. My mind was greatly drawn out in prayer."[5] As he preached in Boston with great conviction borne out of this soul preparation, the Word of God, as a hot knife through butter, cut through intellectual doubt and skepticism to bring many to a knowlege of Christ. Finney's motto was, "Souls at any price and under all circumstances."[6]

Billy Graham's Associate Evangelist, Dr. John Wesley White, has said, "God has given me a furnace in my heart, and the more I pray and preach, the more the fire burns." Touching God on our knees in prayer and obeying God by our witness and proclamation feeds and fans the fire of a passion for souls. And as an earlier and more widely known John Wesley has said, "Get on fire for God and people will come to watch you burn." Wesley would pray four hours a day and once off his knees, he'd exhort his itinerating circuit riders: "You have no other business than to save souls."

The Loss of Compassion

However, we seem to be living in a day when compassion for the lost is dwindling. Some have termed the overall spiritual temperature of the church in this day "lukewarm." J. Oswald Sanders speaks of it in this way, " 'A passion for souls,' as a former generation termed the compassion believers should have for their fellows, is rare in our day. The great mass of Christian people appear to feel not the slightest responsibility for the eternal welfare of their fellow men. The thought that they are their brother's keeper never seems to cross their minds. If they can ensure their own future, that is the extent of their concern.

"Dr. Rowland V. Bingham, founder of the Sudan Interior Mission, referring to this absence of concern for the spiritual welfare of others, said, 'Today this consciousness seems to have almost died out. The natural eye cannot see souls. The ethical veil of society, the cloak of self-righteousness, or the thin veneer of legal morals are impenetrable to the natural sight, and when accompanied with the rosy flush of youth, the glitter of prosperity and the joys of home and social life, it is hard to realize that in the midst of all these are lost souls. Christians, as a whole, do not act as though they believe that anyone is lost.' "[7]

What do you do if the fire has diminished or gone out completely? How do you rekindle the flames of urgency for evangelism? Leighton Ford has aptly asked, "But how about the servant of God who knows the meaning of commitment to Christ but for whom the warm glow of loyalty to Christ may have faded? Staleness always undercuts urgency. If we are bored with our experience of the Christian life, let's face it honestly."[8] Ford and others have suggested several steps to deal with the problem of lost urgency and staleness in our Christian lives:

We should acknowledge the lost urgency to God and to ourselves. Pretending it is not there only prolongs the problem. But admitting it is the first step toward receiving help and recovering our "first love."

We should take time for a spiritual inventory. We should spend part or all of a day alone with God and with His Word, allowing Him to search our heart and being willing to face whatever He brings to mind. It has been well said that sin will keep us from the Word and the Word will keep us from sin. A cold and uncaring heart can often be traced to some lack of obedience in our life. But God will gladly speak to us if we want to hear Him.

J. Wilbur Chapman, the eminent evangelist—who also served as Moderator of the Presbyterian Church, U.S.A.—urged young men concerned about evangelism to "take the Bible and study the spiritual condition of those who are without Christ. 'Take your New Testament,' he counseled, 'and go quietly alone and read a sentence like this, "Whoever believes in Him is not condemned, but whoever does not believe stands condemned already because he has not believed in the name of God's one and only Son" (John 3:18). Then think about it for ten minutes. Put your boy over against it—your girl, your wife, your husband, yourself. Then take this, "He who does not have the Son of God does not have life" (1 John 5:12). I know that a soul thus burdened generally gains its desire.' "[9]

It is often because of this lack of meditation that our compassion grows cold, and the tears of concern are gone from our ministry. The apostle Paul's evangelistic ministry was characterized by tears of compassion. When a young Salvation Army officer wrote to General William Booth to tell him that no souls were being saved under his ministry, Booth wrote back,

"Try tears!" In a biography on the life of A. B. Simpson, founder of the Christian & Missionary Alliance (C&MA), the author writes that one morning Simpson was seen in his study with his arms wrapped around a globe, sobbing tears that men might be saved. Is it any wonder that the C&MA is known for its world missionary outreach?

Seek the help of a trusted Christian friend or a group of believers. There are those who will love you and pray with you, without judging you. They have walked this way also and faced these temptations. Perhaps others need their own sense of urgency rekindled. Covenant together with them and ask that God will not only show you, but use you. It is especially important to spend time with others who have a passion for souls. The effect will be like adding a charcoal briquet to an already glowing fire. Soon the new addition will be raised to the same temperature.

Spend time in prayer. D. L. Moody used to say, "I am a leaky vessel and I need to keep under the tap." The closer we draw to the burning heart of God, the warmer will be our own heart, and the greater our compassion for those whom He died to save.

Charles Finney, "one of the greatest revivalists of all time, used to urge those who coveted this compassion and concern to 'look as it were through a telescope into hell and hear their groans; then to turn the glass upward and look into heaven, and see the saints there in their white robes, and hear them singing the song of redeeming love, and ask yourself, "Is it possible that I could prevail with God to elevate the sinner there?" Do this, and if you are not a wicked man, you will soon have as much of a spirit of prayer as your body can sustain.' "[10]

Obey Christ's command. Sometimes we have to obey whether we feel like it or not. And, interestingly, as we obey Christ's command, urgency and compassion will increase. As Jesus said, "Give, and it shall be given unto you" (Luke 6:38, KJV). Turning on the hot water tap on a cold winter day brings cool water at first; but the longer the water runs, the warmer it becomes. And the pipe through which the water flows takes on the same temperature. The experience of sharing our faith with another and allowing the Word of God and the witness of Christ to be expressed through us has its own dynamic renewing quality in our lives, raising our own "spiritual temperature."

The recovery and maintenance of a compassion for the souls of men is a costly thing. It requires of us hearts that are willing to be broken by Jesus Christ. Dr. J. H. Jowett has written, "The Gospel of a broken heart demands the ministry of bleeding hearts. When our sympathy loses its pang, we can no longer be the servants of the passion. We can never heal the needs we do not feel. Tearless hearts can never be heralds of the passion. We must pity if we would redeem, we must bleed if we would be ministers of the saving blood."[11] It is a truism that there is only one thing worse than prayerless tears. It is tearless prayers.

The earnest prayer of the man or woman who wants to be used by God to win souls could well be expressed in these words,

"Oh, for a passionate passion for souls!
   Oh, for a pity that yearns!
Oh, for a love that loves us unto death!
   Oh, for a fire that burns!"[12]

Reflecting on Amsterdam 83, Billy Graham has written about the urgency of the harvest and the need for more laborers to join in that harvest. "The evangelistic harvest is always urgent. But there seem to be periods of special urgency in history when it can be said with peculiar relevance, the fields 'are ripe for harvest.' I believe that we are now in such a period. Because of technology, this generation is the most critical in modern history, not just for world events but for the advancement of the Kingdom of God. And that should give us a sense of urgency greater than anything that the Church has ever experienced.

"Not only is there a new urgency, but it also means millions of people are searching for answers to the crushing problems and fears they face every day. There is an openness to the Gospel in this generation which we may never see again. Almost every newspaper and every book screams from its pages, 'The harvest is ripe.'

"But 'the laborers are few' in many parts of the world. Their effectiveness, however, can be increased and their fruitfulness multiplied as you become co-laborers with them.

"We do not know how many tomorrows we may have before the final curtain of history is pulled back and Christ comes again. We do not know how many days or years may be left for each of us before God calls us home. We ought to live each day as if it is our last, prayerfully investing the time, talent, and resources with which God has entrusted us, to be a part of His divine strategy for evangelizing the world."[13]

Fulfilling the Great Commission requires much, much more than merely defining the message, determining the task, delineating the principles, or depicting the mission fields, though all are important. It requires men and women motivated by a Holy Spirit-sent passion for souls who, by their obedience will hasten the day when "this gospel . . . shall be preached in all the world; . . . and then shall the end come" (Matthew 24:14, KJV). Will you commit yourself to this task? I pray that you will!

Appendix A
Steps for Developing a Crusade Invitation for Billy Graham Crusades

Step 1:   *Assess Initial Interest*
The first step is to assess the interest in a Billy Graham Crusade by key clergy and judicatory leadership from three major areas of the religious community:

    1. Those traditionally supportive of Crusade evangelism;

    2. Those from principal "mainline" denominations;

    3. Those from the major ethnic group(s). If there is sufficient interest after contacting key individuals representative of these groups, the next step should be the formation of a Temporary Committee.

Step 2:   *Form Temporary Committee*
A small ad hoc group (ten to fifteen persons maximum), composed of key leadership from each of the above-listed three groupings, should be formed. Representation on the committee should reflect the religious structure of the Protestant community and should include both laity and clergy in approxi-

mately a 40 percent to 60 percent ratio, respectively.

The criteria for selection should be:

1. Members are fully supportive of a Billy Graham Crusade invitation;

2. Members represent one of the three groups listed above and have significant peer group influence with their own group or the community at large;

3. Members are willing to attend meetings and pray faithfully for the development of a Crusade invitation.

Note: Usually the Director of Crusades will meet with this ad hoc group, once formed, for an exploratory meeting. From that meeting the group will be offered additional guidance concerning future organizational steps. Future steps usually include the development of an Invitation Committee and the accumulation of letters of invitation.

Step 3: *Develop an Invitation Committee*

The purpose of an Invitation Committee is to reflect to the Billy Graham Team the broad representative Christian support for a Crusade in a community. It also permits every major segment of the Christian community to begin on the ground floor of a Crusade invitation.

This Committee, composed of from 50 to 100 people, depending upon the size and scope of the community, is selected on the basis of the following criteria:

1. They have a demonstrated Christian commitment;

2. They support a Billy Graham Crusade;

3. They represent some aspect of community life—religious, ethnic, professional, educational, business, labor, civic, political.

4. They have respect and influence with their peer group. This is especially important for clergy leadership chosen.

If at all possible, top judicatory leadership from every principal Protestant denomination should be represented on this Committee, as well as pastors of major churches whose support and endorsement is important to the Crusade. Parachurch organization leadership also should be included.

This Committee, which is temporary in nature, will be asked to meet, at most, twice during the next six months to a year to assist in the process of establishing a permanent Crusade organization. Each member will also be asked to write a letter of support and invitation to Billy Graham. These letters should be mailed to a local contact and accumulated for the completion of Step 4. In addition, they will be asked to support, by their prayers and personal comments, the prospect of a Billy Graham Crusade in their community.

Step 4: *Invitational Letters*

Concurrent with the establishment of an Invitation Committee is the accumulation of letters of endorsement and invitation by key leadership from all aspects of the community. A systematic effort should be made to contact top leadership (both Christian and secular) in every occupational grouping to ask for a letter of support. These occupational groupings should consider the professional, educational, business, labor, civic, political, media, and religious areas of the community. Letters by members of the Invitation Committee would be added to letters from community leadership at large, to further round out the support picture. Letters should be sought from all individual clergy throughout the area.

These letters should be written to Billy Graham, but mailed to a local contact to be accumulated and presented to the Crusade Team at some future time.

The above-listed organizational steps give a tangible way to test the interest in a city for a Billy Graham Crusade and to develop that interest in a way that can be expressed meaningfully to members of the Billy Graham Team. The members of the Team are acutely aware of the fact that a successful Crusade can come only through the blessing of God; thus, the primary activity in all aspects of an invitation is to seek prayerfully God's will and encourage others to do the same. Prayer is the most important step. As Billy Graham and the members of the Team face the hundreds of invitations that come to them every year, they are keenly aware of their dependence upon the prayers of God's people to know the leading of God in such decisions.

Appendix B
LOCAL CONGREGATION
Goals for Action—Worksheet

"It is important to set goals too big to be accomplished by human resources alone, and yet small enough so you can believe—with God's help—they can be reached."

1. As you get involved in the Crusade process, decide what you would like to see God do in your church, your community, and yourself because of the Crusade. Take a few moments to write down your thinking on the lines below.

   A. I would like God to accomplish the following things in my church through this Crusade:

   _____

   _____

   _____

   B. I would like God to accomplish the following things in my community through this Crusade:

   _____

   _____

   _____

   C. I would like God to accomplish the following things in me through this Crusade:

   _____

   _____

   _____

2. A Crusade provides a unique opportunity for your church to grow. The first step in growth is to prayerfully establish some goals. Complete the "Now" column with your current church figures and establish some "faith-sized" goals in the "Projected" column to be attained in the next twelve months. One year from now record the "Actual" figures and compare with projected goals.

	Now	Projected	Actual
People attending prayer groups or prayer services	____	____	____
People active in regular personal witnessing	____	____	____
People singing in the church choir	____	____	____
People active in the church's visitation program	____	____	____
People serving as ushers	____	____	____
Church school/Sunday school attendance	____	____	____
Average worship service attendance	____	____	____
Total number of members/ attenders in our church	____	____	____

3. To reach your long-term goals for church growth, you will need to set some short-term goals for your church's involvement in Crusade opportunities.

    It is our goal to see:
    ____of our people *attend* the four-week Christian Life and Witness course, so they can receive training in personal evangelism.
    ____of our people actively *praying* for the Crusade effort, our church, and the community in small prayer groups.

_____of our people, on average, *attending* the Crusade meetings.

_____*new people, brought* to the Crusade to hear the Gospel for the first time as a result of our church's Operation Andrew and visitation programs.

_____of our people *serving* as Counselors/Advisers in the Crusade.

_____of our people *become trained* leaders, guiding new Christians to deeper commitment through Follow-Up Nurture Groups.

Appendix C
The Amsterdam Affirmations

1. We confess Jesus Christ as God, our Lord and Savior, who is revealed in the Bible, which is the infallible Word of God.
2. We affirm our commitment to the Great Commission of our Lord, and we declare our willingness to go anywhere, do anything, and sacrifice anything God requires of us in the fulfillment of that Commission.
3. We respond to God's call to the biblical ministry of the evangelist, and accept our solemn responsibility to preach the Word to all peoples as God gives opportunity.
4. God loves every human being, who, apart from faith in Christ, is under God's judgment and destined for hell.
5. The heart of the biblical message is the good news of God's salvation, which comes by grace alone through faith in the risen Lord Jesus Christ and His atoning death on the cross for our sins.
6. In our proclamation of the Gospel we recognize the urgency of calling all to decision to follow Jesus Christ as Lord and Savior, and to do so lovingly and without coercion or manipulation.
7. We need and desire to be filled and controlled by the Holy Spirit as we bear witness to the Gospel of Jesus Christ, because God alone can turn sin-

ners from their sin and bring them to everlasting life.

8. We acknowledge our obligation, as servants of God, to lead lives of holiness and moral purity, knowing that we exemplify Christ to the Church and to the world.

9. A life of regular and faithful prayer and Bible study is essential to our personal spiritual growth, and to our power for ministry.

10. We will be faithful stewards of all that God gives us, and will be accountable to others in the finances of our ministry, and honest in reporting our statistics.

11. Our families are a responsibility given to us by God, and are a sacred trust to be kept as faithfully as our call to minister to others.

12. We are responsible to the Church, and will endeavor always to conduct our ministries so as to build up the local body of believers and serve the Church at large.

13. We are responsible to arrange for the spiritual care of those who come to faith under our ministry, to encourage them to identify with the local body of believers, and seek to provide for the instruction of believers in witnessing to the Gospel.

14. We share Christ's deep concern for the personal and social sufferings of humanity, and we accept our responsibility as Christians and as evangelists to do our utmost to alleviate human need.

15. We beseech the Body of Christ to join with us in prayer and work for peace in our world, for revival and a renewed dedication to the biblical priority of evangelism in the Church, and for the oneness of believers in Christ for the fulfillment of the Great Commission, until Christ returns.

Appendix D
Basic Concept of Crusade Organization
Billy Graham Evangelistic Association (BGEA)

United evangelistic Crusades, with careful and prayerful organization, services conducted with dignity by a gifted Team, and an extensive program of follow-up, can greatly assist churches in seeking to fulfill their ministry of the Gospel.

Each Crusade, conducted in cooperation with BGEA, begins with, and is carried to completion by, the local church. It is the area churches who invite the evangelist and his Team to the city. These churches provide personnel for the committees to give guidance and action for the months of preparation, the days of the Crusade, and extensive follow-up. It is these churches that receive the joyful benefits of the Crusade, by way of individuals who make commitments to Christ, and spiritual renewal of many of their members.

When Billy Graham accepts an invitation to come to a city, he provides an experienced Team for this venture. This Team includes men who will serve as advisers to the local committee. They will share ideas, materials, and knowledge gathered through more than thirty-five years of experience and study of united Crusade evangelism.

Several basic committees have been found effective and necessary. In adapting the typical Crusade organization to fit the requirements of different cities, sometimes additional committees are organized, and occasionally certain committees are combined or are omitted. Committee membership should be structured in order to give many pastors and laypersons responsibility, thus involving them as a definite part of the Crusade.

Executive Committee

The Executive Committee is the incorporated policy-making body for the Crusade. For this reason it is wise to seek competent legal advice in filing appropriate nonprofit corporation, tax-exempt papers, from the outset. In their responsibility of establishing and carrying out operating policies and the total conduct of the Crusade, the committee carries full financial responsibility for both raising and spending all monies.

Membership should number from 15 to 25 persons, made up of the officers, Chairpersons of the Working Committees, and selected Members-at-Large. This committee should be divided almost equally between ministers and laypersons, and be widely representative of the religious life of the community. Interest in the Crusade ministry and technical ability are equally important factors for committee membership. It is suggested that the Executive Committee meet monthly during the initial planning stages of the Crusade, and more frequently in the three-month period immediately prior to the Crusade meetings.

Chairperson—The Chairperson of the Executive Committee is the key individual for the entire organization. He/She will carry considerable administrative responsibility for the total Crusade program. He/She will represent the Crusade to the public, be the official spokesman at each Crusade meeting, and preside at all Executive sessions. The Chairperson, who may be either a minister or a layperson, should be committed to the Crusade purpose and adequately representative of the Christian community.

Vice-Chairpersons—It is advisable to choose one or more Vice-Chairpersons, who will not chair Working Committees, but be free to assist the Chairperson in administration and supervision of Crusade responsibilities. These persons should be chosen on the basis of their abilities, commitment to the Crusade purpose, and position of leadership in the Christian community. Vice-Chairpersons may be assigned special Crusade projects by the Chairperson, and may also be asked to share the responsibility of supervising several Working Committees. If the Chairperson is a minister, then the Vice-Chairperson or Chairpersons should be laypersons; conversely, if the Chairperson is a layperson, the Vice-Chairpersons should be ministers.

Secretary—The Secretary will record, duplicate, and distribute the minutes of the Executive Committee sessions, notify members of meetings, and give general liaison between the Executive Committee and Working Committees.

Treasurer—The Treasurer will be responsible for the financial records of the Crusade and will, with the Chairperson, make official statements regarding the financial situation. He/She will supervise the setting up of proper bookkeeping techniques, auditing procedures. In consultation with the Executive Committee and the BGEA representative, the Treasurer will help develop the budget.

Members-at-Large—Key leadership, both ministers and laypersons, from the community are often chosen to serve as Members-at-Large. These individuals are usually chosen on the basis of their concern for evangelism and their representation of denominational and interdenominational groups, ethnic communities, civic and public positions, and metropolitan geographic areas. When outlying communities are involved in a Crusade, a liaison representative for that community is often asked to serve as a Member-at-Large, thus providing a voice in Crusade activities.

Administrative Committee

The Administrative Committee is composed of the officers of the Executive Committee and two Members-at-Large also chosen from the Executive Committee. This committee is responsible for making recommendations to, and acting for, the Executive Committee as necessary. Their actions are subject to ratification by the Executive Committee. The Administrative Committee usually meets twice monthly, with one of these scheduled immediately prior to the monthly Executive meeting.

Working Committees

Several Working Committees will be constituted for the detailed planning and execution of the Crusade. In the formative stages the Administrative Committee will make recommendations to the Executive Committee for the Chairpersons of the Working Committees. The elected Chairpersons will, in turn, choose their own committee members, subject to the ratification of the Administrative Committee.

The Chairperson of each Working Committee becomes a member of the Executive Committee. This person must be recognized as a leader who plays an important part in the Christian community and who is considered competent in his/her field, and thus to him/her would fall the natural position of leadership as Chairperson of his/her committee. The Working Committees would cover every phase of a Crusade and divide the responsibilities equally.

General Crusade Committee

In cities where the number of Members-at-Large selected (according to the criteria on Page 193) exceeds ten, it becomes necessary to form a General Crusade Committee. This committee is composed of the Crusade officers, the Working Committee Chairpersons, and all Members-at-Large. Since this committee should include representation from every major segment of the Christian community, its primary purpose is to enhance communications between the Executive Committee and the Christian community. Usually the General Crusade Committee will meet every two months to hear reports of progress from, and offer advisory input to, the Executive Committee. General Crusade Committee meetings are often scheduled to follow immediately after an Executive Committee meeting, or to substitute for the regular monthly meeting of the Executive Committee.

Advisory Committee

In many Crusade situations, but not all, it may be advisable to establish an Advisory Committee or Council of Reference. This is a large committee composed of a widely representative group of clergymen and key community leaders. This group may be considered as a committee of reference, sharing not in administration, but in an advisory capacity. This committee will be kept informed of activities by correspondence and may be called together on one or two occasions prior to, and once during, the early part of the Crusade. This will be done to help interpret the planning and programming of the Crusade to church, community, and civic leadership. The membership of this committee should be encouraged to exercise their advisory capacity with the Executive Committee.

Officers of this committee should be a Chairperson, Vice-Chairperson, and Secretary. If the Chairperson of the Executive Committee is a minister, it is recommended that the Advisory Committee Chairperson be a leading business person. This same principle of balance is true if the Executive Committee Chairperson is a layperson.

BILLY GRAHAM CRUSADE

ORGANIZATION CHART

EXECUTIVE COMMITTEE

ADMINISTRATIVE COMMITTEE

Chairperson _____	Secretary _____
Vice-Chairperson _____	Treasurer _____
Vice-Chairperson _____	Member-at-large _____
Vice-Chairperson _____	Member-at-large _____

B.G.E.A. Team

Evangelist _____

Musicians _____

Director of Crusades _____

Crusade Director _____

Members-at-large	Working Committee Chairpersons
_____	Arrangements _____
_____	Counseling & F-Up _____
_____	Delegations _____
_____	Finance _____
_____	Ladies _____
_____	Laymen _____
_____	Ministers _____
_____	Music _____
_____	Special Outreach _____
_____	Usher _____
_____	Visitation _____
_____	Youth _____

Advisory Committee

Chairperson _____

Co-Chairperson _____

Secretary _____

Appendix E

Sample Crusade Involvement Schedule

Time Prior to
Crusade Meetings

8 months	Executive Committee leadership chosen
7 months	Recruit and organize Mobilizing Committees (Ministers, Women, Youth)
6 months	Crusade Information Seminars (Ministers and Congregational Leaders)
5 months	Congregational Leaders' Seminars (Ministers, Congregational Leaders, Women Leaders, Youth Leaders)
	Formation of Crusade Congregational Committees
3½–4 months	Church Leaders' Rallies (All church leaders attend)
	Recruitment begins
2½–3 months	Christian Life and Witness Classes
	Operation Andrew involvement emphasized
2 months	Follow-up Nurture Group Training
	Men's Prayer Rally
	Women's Prayer Rallies
1 month	Home Prayer Ministry Begins
1–7 days	Crusade Worker Rehearsals
0	Crusade Meetings
Up to 3 months After	Follow-up Activities

Appendix F
Crusade Survey Information

Over several years, Dr. Larry Caillouet surveyed three Crusades involving Billy Graham Association personnel: 1977 Leighton Ford meetings in Huntsville, Alabama; 1980 Billy Graham Crusade in Edmonton, Alberta; and the 1981 Billy Graham Crusade in Baltimore, Maryland.

Huntsville Crusade data confirmed that 93.7 percent of those who attended were primarily influenced by interpersonal media (see Figure 1).

Baltimore data gave the same overall picture with different proportions. Sources of awareness were basically the same (see Figure 1). But mass media were three times as effective in influencing attendance in Baltimore as in Edmonton (30.1 percent versus 9.1 percent).

Differences in mass media effectiveness are best explained by comparing the religiosity of the three cities surveyed (see Figure 2).

Churches which strongly support Crusade evangelism generally have more than one service weekly. In a smaller city, such as Huntsville, where church life is more dominant and supporting churches more common, interpersonal or church network contacts are the first source of information and a stronger influence on Crusade attendance.

In contrast, only 19.9 percent attended church once

Crusade Survey Summary

City	Type Survey	Metro-Area Population	Community Awareness of Crusade	Source of Awareness		Influenced Attendance	
				Mass Media	Interpersonal Media	Mass Media	Interpersonal Media
Huntsville	Community*	150,000	73.8%	60.0%	40.0%	6.3%	93.7%
Edmonton	Community*	600,000	85.6%	78.6%	21.4%	9.1%	90.9%
Baltimore	Community*	2,500,000	88.4%	79.8%	20.2%	30.1%	69.9%
Baltimore	Inquirers**	2,500,000	N/A	38.0%	62.0%	28.2%	71.8%

*Respondents were a scientific sample of the metropolitan area.
**Respondents were a scientific sample of the inquirers at the Crusade.

Figure 1.

Religiosity in 3 Crusade Cities as Measured by Frequency of Church Attendance

City	Less than Once Per Month	Once Per Month	2 or 3 Times Per Month	Once Per Week	More Than Once Per Week
Huntsville (1977)	30.8	11.6	15.2	22.6	19.8
Edmonton (1980)	59.2	9.4	12.2	16.0	3.3
Baltimore (1981)	34.9	13.1	15.5	26.0	10.4

Figure 2.

a week in Edmonton and only 3.3 percent attended more than once a week. Edmonton is four times larger than Huntsville and has much less affinity for Crusade evangelism, so far fewer people were motivated by media information to attend a Crusade. In spite of those differences, interpersonal contact was still the primary factor for influencing attendance.

Baltimore was almost as religious as Huntsville with 36.4 percent attending church at least once a week, but only one-half as many attending church more than once weekly. Baltimore is four times the size of Edmonton and sixteen times the size of Huntsville with a significant non-Protestant religious community. This means that the supporting church network could not as easily permeate the total metropolitan area. The impact of involved churches is usually proportionately less in larger cities than in smaller ones; thus, mass media has a bigger role to play in major metropolitan areas.

Advertising also serves to interest and invite persons from congregations which are not involved in Crusade preparations. We may conclude that the larger the metropolitan area, the more important mass media become in influencing attendance. Still, it is significant to note that even in larger cities, two out of three persons attend a Crusade primarily because of interpersonal influences. Furthermore, nearly three out of four who come forward attend because of personal factors. There is no substitute for individual Christians personally inviting needy persons in their network of relationships.

Since "making disciples" is our goal and this begins when someone responds to the invitation, Crusade inquirers were also surveyed in Baltimore (see Figure 1). The fact that 62 percent were aware of the Crusade because of interpersonal media and 71.8 percent attended because of personal invitation strongly demonstrates the influence of personal factors on those who respond for commitment.

Even more confirming are these facts: 75.6 percent of those inquirers who decided to attend during the week of the Crusade (when advertising and publicity were at their peak) were invited personally by someone and 73.8 percent were given a ride to the meetings. *The personal invitation by involved Christians is absolutely essential for effective Crusade evangelism.*

Publicity emphasis is primarily directed toward the supporting Christian community for most of the preparation period. Communicating with this internal audience is the priority until approximately two weeks prior to the Crusade meetings (see Figure 3).

Timing is crucial in the use of external publicity (see Figure 4). Dr. Caillouet's research reveals that the majority of those who have relatively little church involvement or are infrequent in attendance, decide to attend the meetings during the two weeks just prior to the Crusade, or during the week of the Crusade itself.

During the two weeks prior to the Crusade, advertising and publicity are increased through every

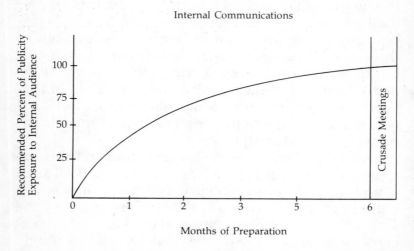

Figure 3.

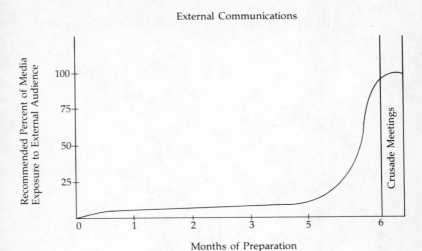

Figure 4.

possible means. The evangelist might hold a press conference and grant media interviews when he arrives in the city. The evangelist's personal opinions expressed in interviews often create additional interest and awareness in the community. It is always easier for Christians to invite their uncommitted friends when the speaker is perceived as an attractive and interesting person.

Appendix G
Local Congregation Resources

American Festival of Evangelism

These four notebooks include invaluable summaries of 200 of the finest programs in North American churches on equipping, discipling, and evangelizing. For more information write:

American Festival of Evangelism
P.O. Box 17093
Washington, D.C. 20041

A Church's Guide to Evangelism

A manual of resources was prepared especially for the churches of New England to promote continuing evangelism following the 1982 New England Billy Graham Crusade. Written by Professor Richard Peace, of Gordon-Conwell Theological Seminary, the manual provides practical and usable insights for local church evangelism. For more information write:

Evangelistic Association of New England
88 Tremont Street
Boston, Massachusetts 02108

Congregational Goals Discovery Plan

The Congregational Goals Discovery Plan is a practical program for helping local congregations determine their needs and opportunities, and establishing goals and a strategy for meeting these needs. Complete with survey forms, worksheets and instruction manuals, the program is applicable to any denomination. For more information write:

Commission on Home Ministries
General Conference Mennonite Church
722 Main Street, Box 347
Newton, Kansas 67114

The Work of an Evangelist

This book is a compendium of major addresses and seminar lectures from Amsterdam '83, which provides both theological and practical insights into preaching evangelism opportunities. It contains extensive material on evangelism and discipleship methods from outstanding Christian leaders from around the world. For more information write:

Grason
1303 Hennepin Avenue
Minneapolis, Minnesota 55403

Single Church Evangelistic Crusade

The Billy Graham Evangelistic Association has prepared an outline for organizing and scheduling a Single Church Evangelistic Crusade. To obtain copies write:

Billy Graham Evangelistic Association
Team Office
P.O. Box 9313
Minneapolis, Minnesota 55440

A Biblical Standard for Evangelists
The Amsterdam Affirmations

Billy Graham has written a commentary based on The Amsterdam Affirmations from the International

Conference for Itinerant Evangelists, July, 1983. The fifteen Affirmations provide guidelines in Christian living, not only for evangelists but for believers everywhere. For more information write:

Grason
1303 Hennepin Avenue
Minneapolis, Minnesota 55403

Selections listed below are used by permission.

Chapter 1

PROCLAMATION: The Evangelist's Ministry and Message

1. "The Evangelist Today," by Stephen F. Olford, in *One Race, One Gospel, One Task*, Vol. II, edited by Carl F. H. Henry and W. Stanley Mooneyham, © 1967 World Wide Publications, Minneapolis, Minnesota, p. 456; The Archbishops' Committee of Inquiry on the Evangelistic Work of the Church, 1918.
2. *A Church's Guide to Evangelism*, by Richard Peace, © 1982 Richard Peace, published by the Evangelistic Association of New England, p. 16.
3. The Lausanne Covenant, © 1974 World Wide Publications, Minneapolis, Minnesota, Clause 4.
4. *The Christian Persuader*, by Leighton Ford, © 1966 Leighton F. S. Ford, Harper & Row, Publishers, Inc., New York, pp. 78–79.
5. *The Apostolic Preaching and Its Development*, by C. H. Dodd, Hodder and Stoughton, London, England, 1936, p. 7.
6. *A Faith to Proclaim*, by James S. Stewart, Charles Scribner's Sons, New York, 1953, pp. 14–15.
7. "The Evangelist and a Torn World," in *The Evangelist and a Torn World: Messages From Amsterdam*, by Billy Graham, © 1983 World Wide Publications, Minneapolis, Minnesota, p. 15.
8. Ibid., pp. 11–12.
9. *Billy Graham: Evangelist to the World*, by John Pollock, © 1979 John Pollock, Harper & Row, Publishers, Inc., New York, p. 316.
10. *The Christian Persuader*, by Leighton Ford, © 1966 Leighton F. S. Ford, Harper & Row, Publishers, Inc., New York, pp. 82–83.
11. Op cit., The Lausanne Covenant, Clause 5.
12. *Effective Evangelism: The Greatest Work in the World*, by George E. Sweazey, © 1953 Harper & Row, Publishers, Inc., New York, p. 173.
13. "Responses to the Savior," by Roger C. Palms, in *Decision*, October, 1982, © 1982 Billy Graham Evangelistic Association, Minneapolis, Minnesota, p. 9.

14. Op cit., The Lausanne Covenant, © 1974 World Wide Publications, Minneapolis, Minnesota, Clause 4.
15. Ibid., Clause 4.

Chapter 2

PURPOSE: *Primary Objectives of Crusade Evangelism*

1. "The Great Commission," by John R. W. Stott, in *One Race, One Gospel, One Task*, edited by Carl F. H. Henry and W. Stanley Mooneyham, © 1967 World Wide Publications, Minneapolis, Minnesota, p. 47.
2. "Discipleship Evangelism," by Waldron Scott, in *Evangelism: The Next Ten Years*, edited by Sherwood Eliot Wirt, copyright © 1978 Sherwood E. Wirt, p. 104; used by permission of Word Books, Publisher, Waco, Texas.
3. Ibid., pp. 105–106.
4. *Leading Your Church in Evangelism*, by Lewis A. Drummond, © 1975 Broadman Press, Nashville, Tennessee, p. 23; first published under the title *Evangelism—The Counter-Revolution*, by Lewis A. Drummond, © 1972 Lewis A. Drummond, Marshall, Morgan & Scott, London, England.
5. Taken from *A Theology of Church Growth*, by George W. Peters, © 1981 The Zondervan Corporation, Grand Rapids, Michigan, p. 207. Used by permission.

Chapter 3

PRINCIPLES: *Keys to Effective Crusade Evangelism*

1. "Prayer and Evangelism," by Armin R. Gesswein, in *Evangelism: The Next Ten Years*, edited by Sherwood Eliot Wirt, copyright © 1978 Sherwood E. Wirt, p. 97; used by permission of Word Books, Publisher, Waco, Texas.
2. Ibid., p. 98.
3. *Your Church Can Grow*, by C. Peter Wagner, © 1976 C. Peter Wagner, Regal Books, G/L Publications, Glendale, California, p. 77.

Chapter 4

PERSPECTIVE: *Crusade Evangelism and the Church*

1. *Your Church Can Be Healthy*, by C. Peter Wagner, © 1979 C. Peter Wagner, Abingdon Press, Nashville, Tennessee, p. 117.

2. *The Christian Persuader*, by Leighton Ford, © 1966 Leighton F. S. Ford, Harper & Row, Publishers, Inc., New York, p. 81.
3. "Lay Training for Evangelism," by Maurice A. P. Wood, in *Evangelism: The Next Ten Years*, edited by Sherwood Eliot Wirt, copyright © 1978 Sherwood E. Wirt, p. 83; used by permission of Word Books, Publisher, Waco, Texas.
4. *Your Church Can Grow*, by C. Peter Wagner, © 1976 C. Peter Wagner, Regal Books Division, G/L Publications, Glendale, California, p. 75.

Chapter 5

PARTICIPATION: *Involving the Local Church*

1. "Contemporary Practices of Evangelism," by G. W. Peters, in *Let the Earth Hear His Voice*, edited by J. D. Douglas, © 1975 World Wide Publications, Minneapolis, Minnesota, p. 182.
2. "What Ten Years Have Taught Me," by Billy Graham, in *The Christian Century*, February 17, 1960, p. 186.
3. "The Biblical Mandate to Evangelise," by Billy Graham, in *Evangelism Alert*, edited by Gilbert W. Kirby, © 1972 World Wide Publications, London, England, p. 76.
4. Taken from *Cooperative Evangelism*, by Robert O. Ferm, © 1958 Zondervan Publishing House, Grand Rapids, Michigan, p. 94. Used by permission.
5. Ibid., p. 93.
6. "The Evangelist and His Preaching," in *The Evangelist and a Torn World: Messages From Amsterdam*, by Billy Graham, © 1983 World Wide Publications, Minneapolis, Minnesota, p. 29.
7. *I Want My Church to Grow*, by C. B. Hogue, © 1977 Broadman Press, Nashville, Tennessee, p. 66.
8. *Basic New Testament Evangelism*, by Faris Daniel Whitesell, © 1949, Zondervan Publishing House, Grand Rapids, Michigan, p. 144.
9. Taken from *Basic Evangelism*, by C. E. Autrey, © 1959 Zondervan Publishing House, Grand Rapids, Michigan, p. 63. Used by permission.

Chapter 7

PROMOTION: *Factors That Influence Crusade Attendance*

*"It Took a Miracle," by John W. Peterson, © copyright 1948, renewal 1976 by John W. Peterson Music Co. All rights re-

served. International copyright secured. Used by permission of Good Life Publications, Inc., Scottsdale, Arizona 85258.

Chapter 8

PRESERVATION: Turning Decisions Into Disciples

1. *Those Who Came Forward*, by Curtis Mitchell, © 1966 Curtis Mitchell, Chilton Books, Chilton Company, Publishers, Philadelphia, Pennsylvania, and Ambassador Books, Ltd., Toronto, Ontario, Canada, p. 11.
2. *Church Growth and the Whole Gospel: A Biblical Mandate*, by C. Peter Wagner, © 1981 C. Peter Wagner, Harper & Row, Publishers, Inc., New York, p. 57.
3. "Discipleship Evangelism," by Waldron Scott, in *Evangelism: The Next Ten Years*, edited by Sherwood Eliot Wirt, copyright © 1978 Sherwood E. Wirt, p. 106; used by permission of Word Books, Publisher, Waco, Texas.
4. *Billy Graham: The Authorized Biography*, by John Pollock, © 1966 John Pollock, McGraw-Hill Book Company, New York, p. 105.
5. Ibid., pp. 105–106.
6. *The Christian Persuader*, by Leighton Ford, © 1966 Leighton F. S. Ford, Harper & Row, Publishers, Inc., New York, p. 85.
7. *Effective Evangelism: The Greatest Work in the World*, by George E. Sweazey, © 1953 Harper & Row, Publishers, Inc., New York, p. 206.

Chapter 9

PRODUCT: Lasting Benefits for the Local Church

1. *The Impact of Billy Graham Crusades: Are They Effective?* by Lewis A. Drummond, © 1982 World Wide Publications, Minneapolis, Minnesota, p. 10.
2. Ibid., p. 7.
3. "Awakening in New England," by Roger C. Palms, in *Decision*, September, 1982, © 1982 Billy Graham Evangelistic Association, Minneapolis, Minnesota, p. 9.
4. *New England Church Life*, published by Evangelistic Association of New England, Boston, Massachusetts, December, 1982, p. 11.
5. "Greater Boston: Rejoicing Even in the Rain," by Roger C. Palms, in *Decision*, October, 1982, © 1982 Billy Graham Evan-

gelistic Association, Minneapolis, Minnesota, p. 9.

6. Quoted in "Islanders See More Enthusiasm and Service in the Wake of Providence Rally," by Sally C. Cameron, in *New England Church Life*, published by Evangelistic Association of New England, Boston, Massachusetts, June, 1982, p. 15.

7. Op cit., *New England Church Life*, December, 1982, p. 11.

8. Excerpts from "Do Billy Graham's 'Crusades' Have Lasting Effect?" by Stanley High, *Reader's Digest*, September, 1955, © 1955 The Reader's Digest Association, Inc., Pleasantville, New York, p. 5 (reprint). Reprinted with permission.

9. *Church Leaders' Handbook*, © 1982 Billy Graham Evangelistic Association, Minneapolis, Minnesota, preface.

10. Op cit., *New England Church Life*, June, 1982, p. 15.

11. Drummond, op cit., p. 12.

12. Ibid., pp. 8–9.

13. Ibid., p. 19.

14. Op cit., *Decision*, October, 1982, p. 9.

15. Ibid., p. 9.

16. Op cit., *Church Leaders' Handbook*, p. 18.

17. *The Christian Persuader*, by Leighton Ford, © 1966 Leighton F. S. Ford, Harper & Row, Publishers, Inc., New York, p. 97.

18. Stanley High, op cit., p. 2 (reprint).

19. Ibid., p. 2 (reprint).

Chapter 10

POTENTIAL: These Principles Can Work for You

1. Lecture at a convocation on evangelism, Stanford University.

2. "What Makes a Church Grow?" by O. D. Emery, in *Church Growth: America* magazine, March-April, 1978, reprinted in *The Pastor's Church Growth Handbook*, edited by Win Arn, © 1979 Church Growth Press, The Institute for American Church Growth, Pasadena, California, p. 137.

3. "Goal Setting: A Key to the Growth of the Body," by C. Peter Wagner.

4. *Creative Church Administration*, by Lyle E. Schaller and Charles A. Tidwell, Abingdon, Nashville, Tennessee, pp. 150–153.

5. Emery, op cit., p. 138.

6. *Your Church Can Grow*, by C. Peter Wagner, © 1976 C. Peter Wagner, Regal Books, G/L Publications, Ventura, California, p. 75.

7. *Your Spiritual Gifts Can Help Your Church Grow*, by C. Peter Wagner, © 1979 C. Peter Wagner, Regal Books, G/L Publi-

cations, Ventura, California, p. 172.

8. Ibid., p. 177.
9. *Good News Is for Sharing*, by Leighton Ford, © 1977 David C. Cook Publishing Co., Elgin, Illinois, p. 83.
10. "A Winsom Witness," by David Allan Hubbard, in "Today's Christian," September, 1976, p. 2.

Chapter 11

PERSON: The Servant God Uses

1. *The Holy Spirit*, by Billy Graham, copyright © 1978 Billy Graham, pp. 121–122; used by permission of Word Books, Publisher, Waco, Texas.
2. "Billy Graham: An Appreciation," by Harold John Ockenga; in *Evangelism: The Next Ten Years*, edited by Sherwood Eliot Wirt, copyright © 1978 Sherwood E. Wirt, pp. 12–13; used by permission of Word Books, Publisher, Waco, Texas.
3. *The Holy Spirit*, op cit., p. 220.

Chapter 12

PASSION: The Urgency to Evangelize

1. *The Christian Persuader*, by Leighton Ford, © 1966 Leighton F. S. Ford, Harper & Row, Publishers, Inc., New York, pp. 13–14.
2. "The Urgency and Relevancy of Evangelism," by Ishaya S. Audu, in *One Race, One Gospel, One Task*, edited by Carl F. H. Henry and W. Stanley Mooneyham, © 1967 World Wide Publications, Minneapolis, Minnesota, p. 119.
3. "The Biblical Mandate to Evangelise," by Billy Graham, in *Evangelism Alert*, edited by Gilbert W. Kirby, © 1972 World Wide Publications, London, England, p. 76.
4. Taken from *Charles G. Finney*, by Basil Miller, © 1961, 1969 Basil Miller, transferred to Zondervan Publishing House, p. 27; used by permission of Zondervan Publishing House, Grand Rapids, Michigan.
5. Ibid., p. 105.
6. Ibid., p. 99.
7. *Effective Evangelism: The Divine Art of Soul-Winning*, by J. Oswald Sanders, © 1982 J. Oswald Sanders (original title: *The Divine Art of Soul-Winning*), STL Books, Bromley, Kent, England, pp. 9–10.

8. *The Christian Persuader*, op cit., p. 33.
9. *Effective Evangelism*, op cit., pp. 18–19.
10. Ibid., p. 19.
11. Ibid., p. 13.
12. "Oh, for a Pentecost!" in *The Best Loved Religious Poems*, compiled by James Gilchrist Lawson, © 1933 Fleming H. Revell Company, Old Tappan, New Jersey, p. 176.
13. *Billy Graham—A Vision Imparted: A Pictorial Report*, by Dave Foster, © 1984 World Wide Publications, Minneapolis, Minnesota, pp. 93–94.